Wonder
Classroom Questions

A SCENE BY SCENE TEACHING GUIDE

Amy Farrell

SCENE BY SCENE
ENNISKERRY, IRELAND

Copyright © 2017 by Scene by Scene.

Without limiting the rights under copyright, this book is sold subject to the condition that it shall not, by way of trade or otherwise be lent, resold, hired out, reproduced, stored on or introduced into a retrieval system, or transmitted, in any form or by any means (electronic, mechanical, photocopying, recording or otherwise), or otherwise circulated, without the publisher's prior consent, in any form other than that in which it is published and without a similar condition, including this condition, being imposed on the subsequent publisher.

All rights reserved. No part of this publication may be recorded or transmitted in any form or by any means electronic, mechanical, photocopying, recording or otherwise without the proper consent of the publisher.

The publisher reserves the right to change, without notice, at any time, the specification of this product, whether by change of materials, colours, format, text revision or any other characteristic.

Scene by Scene
Enniskerry
Wicklow, Ireland.
www.scenebysceneguides.com

Wonder Classroom Questions by Amy Farrell.
ISBN 978-1-910949-67-2

Contents

Part One - August	1
1. Ordinary	3
2. Why I Didn't Go To School	5
3. How I Came to Life	7
4. Christopher's House	11
5. Driving	13
6. Paging Mr. Tushman	16
7. Nice Mrs. Garcia	18
8. Jack Will, Julian and Charlotte	20
9. The Grand Tour	22
10. The Performance Space	24
11. The Deal	26
12. Home	28
13. First Day Jitters	30
14. Locks	32
15. Around the Room	34
16. Lamb to the Slaughter	36
17. Choose Kind	38
18. Lunch	40
19. The Summer Table	42
20. One to Ten	44
21. Padawan	46
22. September	48
23. Jack Will	50

24. Mr. Browne's October Precept	52
25. Apples	54
26. Halloween	56
27. School Pictures	58
28. The Cheese Touch	60
29. Costumes	62
30. The Bleeding Scream	64
31. Names	66
Part Two - Via	69
32. A Tour of the Galaxy	70
33. Before August	72
34. Seeing August	74
35. August Through the Peephole	76
36. High School	78
37. Major Tom	80
38. After School	82
39. The Padawan Bites the Dust	84
40. An Apparition at the Door	86
41. Breakfast	88
42. Genetics 101	90
43. The Punnett Square	92
44. Out with the Old	94
45. October 31	96
46. Trick or Treat	98
47. Time to Think	100
Part Three - Summer	103
48. Weird Kids	104
49. The Plague	106
50. The Halloween Party	108

51. November	110
52. This Kid is Rated R	112
53. The Egyptian Tomb	114
Part Four - Jack	116
54. The Call	117
55. Carvel	119
56. Why I Changed My Mind	121
57. Four Things	123
58. Ex-Friends	125
59. Snow	127
60. Fortune Favors the Bold	129
61. Private School	131
62. In Science	133
63. Partners	135
64. Detention	137
65. Season's Greetings	139
66. Letters, Emails, Facebook, Texts	141
67. Back from Winter Break	145
68. The War	147
69. Switching Tables	149
70. Why I Didn't Sit With August the First Day of School	151
71. Sides	153
72. August's House	155
73. The Boyfriend	157
Part Five - Justin	159
74. Olivia's Brother	160
75. Valentine's Day	162
76. Our Town	164
77. Ladybug	166

78. The Bus Stop	168
79. Rehearsal	170
80. Bird	172
81. Universe	174
Part Six - August	176
82. North Pole	177
83. The Auggie Doll	179
84. Lobot	182
85. Hearing Brightly	184
86. Via's Secret	186
87. My Cave	188
88. Goodbye	190
89. Daisy's Toys	192
90. Heaven	194
91. Understudy	196
92. The Ending	198
Part Seven - Miranda	200
93. Camp Lies	201
94. School	204
95. What I Miss Most	208
96. Extraordinary, but No One There to See	210
97. The Performance	213
98. After the Show	215
Part Eight - August	217
99. The Fifth Grade Nature Retreat	218
100. Known For	220
101. Packing	222
102. Daybreak	225
103. Day One	227

104. The Fairgrounds	229
105. Be Kind to Nature	231
106. The Woods are Alive	233
107. Alien	235
108. Voices in the Dark	239
109. The Emperor's Guard	241
110. Sleep	243
111. Aftermath	245
112. Home	247
113. Bear	250
114. The Shift	252
115. Ducks	254
116. The Last Precept	256
117. The Drop Off	258
118. Take Your Seats Everyone	260
119. A Simple Thing	262
120. Awards	264
121. Floating	266
122. Pictures	268
123. The Walk Home	270
124. Appendix	272
Further Questions	274

Part One - August

1. Ordinary

Summary

Although the speaker feels ordinary, he knows he is different to other kids because of how he looks.

People stare at him wherever he goes.

He wishes he had a normal face, that no one ever noticed.

He has become good at pretending he does not see people's reactions when they see him. His parents are also very good at this, but his sister Via is not. She gets annoyed when people are rude.

The narrator's name is August. He does not describe what he looks like, saying that whatever the reader is thinking, he looks worse.

Questions

1. What ordinary things does the speaker do?

2. How do people react when they see him?

3. If he found a magic lamp, what would he wish for?

4. What is Via not good at?
   What does this tell you about her personality?

5. How do Via and August's parents view him?

6. What is your response to this opening chapter?
   What questions would you like to ask?
   How does it make you feel?
   Do you want to read on?
   Give reasons for your answer.

2. Why I Didn't Go To School

Summary

August is starting the fifth grade next week. He has never attended school before, because of all the surgeries he has had, and is very scared about going.

His mom homeschooled him until now. She used to be a children's-book illustrator.

August's good friends are Christopher, Zachary and Alex. He has known them since they were babies and they are used to him.

Christopher has moved away and Zachary and Alex have new friends from school.

Questions

1. How does August feel about going to school?

2. What do people assume is the reason he has not gone to school before now?

3. What is the real reason he has not attended school before now?

4. Who has taught August up to now?

5. Who are August's friends?
   Do they sound like good friends to you?

6. August mentions birthday invitations in this chapter. Why, do you think, are party invitations important to him?

3. How I Came to Life

Summary

August loves when his mother tells the story of him being born because it is funny.

The doctors realised there was something wrong with his face about two months before he was born, but they did not think it was going to be bad.

One of the nurses in the delivery room on the night August was born kept farting. It is this detail that makes him laugh.

The room went very quiet when August was born. The nice nurse rushed him out of the room before his mother got to see him.

The farting nurse restrained his mother. The doctor fainted.

The farting nurse turned out to be a very nice woman, staying with August's mother the whole time.

His mother was told all about him before she saw him for the first time. She says that when she looked down into his tiny mushed-up face, all she could see was how pretty his eyes were.

August ends the chapter by saying that his family are all really good-looking.

Questions

1. What did the doctors realise two months before August was born?

2. What was funny about one of the nurses in the delivery room on the night that August was born?

3. What happened when August was born?

4. What did the nice nurse do with August?
   Why did she do this, do you think?

5. What did the farting nurse do?

6. What happened to the doctor?

7. August says that when his mother tells this story it is very funny.
   Does it sound funny to you?

8. Was the farting nurse kind to his mother?

9. When she first saw him, what did August's mother notice about him?
   What does this tell you about her?

10. August ends this chapter by telling us that his family are all good-looking.
    Why does he do this?
    Is this an impotant detail?

11. How must August's parents have felt after his birth? How would you feel in their position?

4. Christopher's House

Summary

August misses playing with his friend Christopher. He moved away three years ago.

Last spring, when his family were visiting Christopher's, he overheard his mom talking about him going to school in the fall.

He did not think he was ready to go and neither did his dad.

He knew that his parents would argue about it later. He wanted his dad to win the fight, though a part of him knew that his mom was right.

Questions

1. What used August and Christopher play together?

2. What does August overhear his mother telling Lisa?

3. Why does August's mother want him to go to school?

4. Why won't he go to his sister's school?
   Do you believe this reason? Why/why not?

5. What opinion does his dad have about August going to school?

6. What babyish thing does August do in this chapter?
   Why does he act like this, in your view?

7. Which parent do you agree with on the matter of August going to school?
   Give reasons for your answer.

8. How would you feel about starting school, if you were August?
   Give reasons for your answer.

5. Driving

Summary

August and Via sleep on the drive home while their parents talk.

August wakes up and overhears his parents' conversation. His mother argues that he needs to deal with his reality, while his father says he will be like a lamb to the slaughter.

August says that everyone will stare at him in school and starts to cry.

His mother assures him that he does not have to go to school if he does not want to. She says that the principal is very keen to meet him though.

August is not happy to hear that his parents met with the principal last year and did not tell him about it.

He guesses that a lady who came to his house to test him was also from the school.

August does not want to go to school.

While she knows it will be a challenge, his mother thinks that going to school would be good for him.

August's dad makes fun of the principal's name and August starts to smile and laugh.

Via wakes up and asks who Mr. Tushman is. August tells her he is the principal of his new school.

Questions

1. Why is there a towel wrapped around the seatbelt?
   What does this tell you about August?

2. What are August's parents discussing when he wakes up?
   What opposing views do they have?

3. Why does August start to cry?
   What do his parents say to reassure him?

4. What have August's parents told the school principal about him?

5. Why is August annoyed when he hears his parents had a tour of the school last year?

6. What did August's mother lie to him about?
   Do you understand what made her lie to him here?
   Does this excuse the lie?

7. What reasons does August's mother have for thinking that school would be good for him?
   Do you agree with her?

8. How does August's dad make him smile?

9. What are August's parents like, based on what you have learned of them so far?

6. Paging Mr. Tushman

Summary

August feels giggly when he meets Mr. Tushman, thinking of his dad's jokes.

Mr. Tushman looks right at August and smiles and shakes his hand. He tells him that his parents have told him a lot about August, and begins a tour of the school for him.

Questions

1. What makes August giggly when he goes to meet Mr. Tushman?

2. How does Mr. Tushman treat August when he meets him?
   What does this tell you about Mr. Tushman?

3. What have August's parents told Mr. Tushman about him?

4. Why is August a bit put out that they are going on a tour of the school, do you think?

5. What are your first impressions of Mr. Tushman?

6. In this chapter August says he has a bad habit of mumbling.
   Why is this a problem for him?

7. Nice Mrs. Garcia

Summary

August hides behind his mom as they walk to Mrs. Garcia's office.

When she meets August her eyes drop for a split second, but she keeps smiling and is nice to him.

August does not look at her, but looks at her stuff instead.

August's mom comments on a cute baby picture on her desk and Mrs. Garcia assures her that they will take good care of August.

Questions

1. Why does August hide behind his mom as they walk? Do you feel sorry for him here?

2. How does Mrs. Garcia react to meeting August? Is she nice to him?

3. Why doesn't August look at her while she is speaking to him?

4. What is significant about the baby picture on Mrs. Garcia's desk?

5. Why, do you think, does Mrs. Garcia squeeze August's mom's hand?

8. Jack Will, Julian and Charlotte

Summary

August and his mother go to Mr. Tushman's office. August is laughing when he hears kids' voices outside. Mr. Tushman has asked them to show August around, as they will be in his homeroom this year.

Jack Will, Julian and Charlotte are introduced to August.

He is mad with his mom, but sees how scared she is, so does not say anything, but follows the others.

Questions

1. What does August like about Mr. Tushman's office?

2. Why does August laugh in Mr. Tushman's office?

3. How does August react when he hears kids' voices? Can you explain this reaction?

4. Why has Mr. Tushman asked some students to come in? Does this sound like a good idea to you?

5. How do the children behave when they meet August?

6. Why is August's mother so nervous?

7. How would you feel if you were August?

8. How would you feel if you were one of the other kids showing him around?

9. The Grand Tour

Summary

The children walk upstairs in silence. Julian opens door 301 and tells August this is where they will have homeroom. Julian does not look at August while he talks. He points out the science lab and Jack Will tells him to let August see inside.

Julian and Charlotte bicker over small details. Julian stays clear of August, not wanting to accidentally touch him.

Julian points out everything in the lab, assuming that August does not know what anything is.

Jack Will asks August if he can talk. He answers that he can and asks what homeroom is.

Questions

1. What are your first impressions of Julian, Charlotte and Jack Will?

2. What makes Julian think that August does not know what anything is?

3. How do these kids treat August? Are they kind and welcoming?

10. The Performance Space

Summary

Charlotte talks about her performance in 'Oliver' as they go towards the auditorium. Julian makes fun of what she is saying and she calls him obnoxious.

August says he is taking the science elective. Julian asks him why he thinks he will be smart enough for it.

Charlotte says he was homeschooled, but Julian says August's mother is not a real teacher.

Julian asks August if he was in a fire, wanting to know what happened to his face. Charlotte calls Julian rude and Jack tells him to shut up.

Jack brings August to the library and holds the door open, looking him in the face. August smiles at him and Jack smiles back and calls Julian a jerk. He tells August that he needs to talk.

August corrects Julian's use of the word 'supposedly'.

As they walk to the stairs, Julian cuts in front of August, making him stumble.

Questions

1. What does Charlotte talk about when they go to the auditorium?

2. In the auditorium, Charlotte calls Julian obnoxious.
   What does this word mean?
   Is she right about Julian's behaviour?
   Include examples to support your view.

3. How do Charlotte and Julian respond when August says he is taking the science elective?
   What does this tell you about each of them?

4. Is Julian rude to ask August questions about his face like this?

5. Why is it significant that Jack Will smiles at August as they leave the auditorium?

6. What advice does Jack Will give August?

7. How has this chapter developed your view of Julian, Charlotte and Jack Will?
   What have you learned about them?

8. Are you impressed by the facilities in August's new school?
   Give reasons for your answer.

11. The Deal

Summary

They return to Mr. Tushman's office. Julian is chatty with August's mom. She asks about a baby chick in the science lab.

Charlotte offers to show August the art room, but he signals to his mother that he wants to leave by mentioning that they need to collect his sister. She is also visiting her new school today.

They say goodbye quickly and leave.

Questions

1. Comment on the way Julian chats with August's mom. Does this tell you anything about him?

2. Why does August wish that his mom would not talk about the baby chick?
   Do you understand what makes him feel this way?

3. How does August let his mother know that he wants to leave?

4. What school is Via going to?

5. Why is August so eager to leave?
   Would you feel the same way, in his position?

12. Home

Summary

August does not talk to his mom about visiting the school until they get home.

He throws himself onto his bed, feeling mixed emotions. He rubs his dog while his mother asks him questions.

She thought that Julian was especially nice, but August says he was the least nice.

She realises that Julian is the type of kid who behaves differently in front of adults.

She is shocked when August tells her what Julian asked about his face.

She tells him that he does not have to go to school, but he says that he wants to.

Questions

1. What does August do when he gets home?
   Can you explain how he is feeling?

2. What does his mother realise about Julian?

3. How does his mom react when she hears what Julian said to August about his face?
   How would you feel in her position?

4. At the end of this chapter, August says he wants to go to school.
   Why does he feel this way, do you think?

13. First Day Jitters

Summary

August is nervous on his first day of school.

After the school visit, his mother now thinks that he should not go, while his dad is impressed by how he handled Julian and thinks that he should.

His family walk with him to school and each of them hugs him before he goes in.

Questions

1. How is August feeling on his first day of school?

2. August's parents have "reversed sides" on whether he should go to school.
   What has made them change their minds?

3. Are August's family supportive on his first day?
   Include examples in your answer.

4. How would you be feeling if you were Via?

5. How would you be feeling if you were August's parents?

14. Locks

Summary

August goes straight to his classroom and sits at the back. No one sits next to him.

Charlotte gives him a wave and says hello. Julian ignores him.

Jack Will arrives and sits next to August.

Ms. Petosa begins handing out class schedules and combination locks.

Henry Joplin does not have a seat, but is reluctant to sit beside August when this place is allocated to him. He places his backpack on the desk, like a barrier.

When all the folders are handed out, Ms. Petosa tells the students to practise opening their combination locks.

Henry cannot get his to open, but August does not help him.

Questions

1. What does August do when he goes into school?

2. How do Charlotte and Julian greet August? Does this tell you anything about them?

3. Jack takes the seat next to August. How does this make you feel? Does this tell you anything about Jack?

4. How does August know that Ms. Petosa has seen him?

5. What will Ms. Petosa spend the class doing?

6. How can August tell that Henry Joplin does not want to sit beside him?

7. Does August like Ms. Petosa, do you think?

8. Why doesn't August help Henry with his lock? Would you, if you were August?

9. How would you be feeling, if you were August on his first morning in school?

15. Around the Room

Summary

Ms. Petosa talks about herself a little and then asks the students to think of two things they want other people to know about them.

Ms. Petosa begins with Julian.

Questions

1. What activity does Ms. Petosa set for the group?
   Do you enjoy this kind of activity?
   Give reasons for your answer.

2. What is your impression of Julian, based on his behaviour in this chapter?

16. Lamb to the Slaughter

Summary

August mentions his sister, Via, and his dog, when it is his turn to speak.

Julian asks August if the braid in his hair is a Padawan thing, a reference to Star Wars. Julian asks if he likes Darth Sidious, a character whose face is deformed by Sith lightning. No-one else seems to get this comment, but August knows that it is intentional.

Questions

1. What does the expression, "Like a lamb to the slaughter" mean?
   How might it apply to August?

2. Why does Julian make a comment about Darth Sidious? What is your response to this?

3. Why doesn't Julian get in trouble here?

17. Choose Kind

Summary

August hurries to English class and sits down the back, where Jack joins him.

Mr. Browne's lesson is to do with precepts, rules about really important things.

His September precept is that when given the choice between being right or being kind, to choose being kind. At the end of the month, the class will have to write an essay about this.

Writing down this precept, August realises that he will enjoy school, no matter what.

Questions

1. What does August do when the bell rings?
   Is his first day going well, do you think?

2. What is a precept?

3. According to Mr. Browne, what is the most important thing of all?
   Do you agree with him?

4. What is Mr. Browne's September precept?
   What is your response to this precept?

5. What is August's response to Mr. Browne's September precept?
   Can you explain what makes him respond like this?

6. Does Mr. Browne seem like a good teacher?
   Give reasons for your answer.

18. Lunch

Summary

The cafeteria is full of noisy kids at lunch time. August sits at an empty table and takes out his packed lunch.

He knows that people are staring at him and talking about him.

He hates how he eats because it is so weird looking, despite the surgeries he has had.

Questions

1. What is lunch time like in the cafeteria?

2. How do the other students react to seeing August at lunch time?
   How does this make him feel?
   What is your response to this?

3. Why does August hate the way he eats?
   How did he realise this?
   Do you feel sorry for August here?

19. The Summer Table

Summary

A girl he has never seen before joins August for lunch. Her name is Summer. Her friend asks her to come back to their table, but she declines, choosing to stay with August.

She says their names match and they spend lunch time coming up with other people with summer names who could join them at their summer table.

Questions

1. Describe the girl who joins August at his table.
   Why does her friend follow her over?
   Why doesn't her friend sit with August?

2. Does Summer seem nice to you?
   Give reasons for your answer.

3. Would you have joined August, in Summer's position?
   Give a reason for your answer.

20. One to Ten

Summary

August's mom is in the habit of asking him how things feel on a scale of one to ten. This is from when he had his jaw surgery and could not speak. Now they are in the habit of using the one-to-ten scale for anything that hurts.

After school, he scores the day with a five, which is better than his mom had hoped for. He tells her that everyone was nice, but feels kind of mad at her, without knowing why.

He tells her he knows Summer from lunch. His mom says she is pretty and August says they are kind of like Beauty and the Beast.

Questions

1. Where does the one-to-ten scale for how much something hurts come from?

2. How does August score the day?
   What is his mother's response to this?

3. Does August tell his mom everything about his day?
   What does he keep from her?

4. As they head home, August feels kind of mad at his mom. Can you explain why August feels like this?

5. What comment does August make about him and Summer?
   How must this comment make his mom feel?

6. Has his first day gone well?
   Give a reason for your answer.

21. Padawan

Summary

That night August cuts off his braid, to Via's disbelief.

His dad comes to tuck him in and asks him if his day was really ok, as he has been very quiet all night.

His mom reads to him and he starts to cry. He asks her why he has to be so ugly.

She kisses him and comforts him, but he knows that her words cannot change his face.

Questions

1. How does Via react when August cuts off his braid?

2. Why is August so quiet all evening, in your opinion?

3. Why does August start to cry while his mother reads to him?
   How does this part of the story make you feel?
   Explain your answer fully.

22. September

Summary

The rest of September is hard for August. School takes up all of his time.

He finds the other students' staring difficult. He knows that people are talking about him.

He does not blame them for acting this way, knowing they are just being normal, dumb kids.

After a month, the entire school has got used to his face.

Questions

1. Why is the rest of September hard for August?

2. Why does he find school awful in the beginning?
   If you were August, would you quit school because of this?

3. Does August blame the other kids for treating him this way?
   What does this tell you about August?

4. How long does it take the kids in August's school to get used to his face?

5. At the end of this chapter August makes the point that of all the kids in his school, none of them look like him. Does he feel isolated because of how he looks, do you think?
   Is there anything the school could do to address this?

6. Is it important to feel there are people like you in your school?
   Explain your point of view.

23. Jack Will

Summary

August sits with Jack in homeroom, English, history, computer, music and science. He also walks to classes with Jack.

Jack asks August whether he ever wants to beat up the kids who stare.

He asks August about plastic surgery.

August tells him his face looks like this *after* plastic surgery. The pair laugh so much that the teacher makes them move seats.

Questions

1. What classes does August sit with Jack in?

2. The teachers put Jack sitting with August in every class they share.
   Are they expecting a lot from Jack, do you think?

3. What do August and Jack laugh about in class?
   Does this surprise you?

4. Is Jack a good friend to August?
   Include examples in your answer.

24. Mr. Browne's October Precept

Summary

Mr. Browne's October precept is 'Your Deeds Are Your Monuments', an idea taken from ancient Egypt.

August understands this to mean that our actions outlast our mortality. These actions become the memories that people have of us.

Questions

1. What is Mr. Browne's October precept?

2. Where does this idea come from?

3. What does August understand this precept to mean? Do you think he understands it correctly?

4. Do you think that this precept is true?

25. Apples

Summary

August wants to have a bowling party for his birthday, and invite everyone in his homeroom, plus Summer.

A few weeks later he asks his mom who is coming to the party. She tells him Jack Will, Summer, Reid Kingsley and both Maxes will be there, and a couple of others will come too, if they can.

August wants to know why other people cannot make it, but his mother says they sent out the evites kind of late.

He still has a great time at his birthday. His friend Christopher and Aunt Kate and Uncle Po come as well as the small group of kids from school.

Questions

1. How does August want to celebrate his birthday?

2. Why does he want to invite so many kids?

3. Who will be coming to his party?
   What is his reaction to this?

4. August's mother says they sent out the evites kind of late. Do you think this is the reason that so few kids come to his party?

5. Does August enjoy his birthday party?
   Give reasons for your answer.

26. Halloween

Summary

Summer asks August who he plans to dress up as for Halloween. He is planning to be Boba Fett.

Summer and August have lunch together everyday.

She wants to dress as a unicorn for Halloween, but thinks it is too dorky.

August encourages her not to care what other people think. She decides to be a unicorn for the Halloween Parade and a Goth girl for school.

She tells August that the thing she likes best about him is that she feels she can tell him anything.

Questions

1. Who is August going to dress as for Halloween?
   Do you know anything about this character?

2. Does August see much of Summer in school?

3. What does Summer want to dress up as?
   What is stopping her from going with this choice?

4. What does she decide on?

5. What does Summer like best about August?

27. School Pictures

Summary

August does not want to have his school portrait taken and his mom does not make him.

He does have to be part of the class picture though. He is sure the photographer thinks he ruined the picture.

Questions

1. What point is the author making in this chapter?

2. Following on from the previous chapter, how does this section change the mood?
   What is the effect of this?

28. The Cheese Touch

Summary

August realises that although kids in school are getting used to him, nobody actually touches him.

Ximena Chin has a panic attack in dance class when the teacher tries to make her be August's partner.

In science elective, Tristan jerks his hand and knocks everything on the floor when August accidentally bumps his hand. He then goes and washes his hands immediately.

August compares himself to the Cheese Touch in *Diary of a Wimpy Kid*. He is the old mouldy cheese no-one wants to touch.

Questions

1. What does August notice about the other kids at school?

2. How does Ximena Chin react when she is paired with August for dance class?

3. What were they doing in science elective yesterday?

4. What does Mr. Rubin notice?

5. What does Tristan do when August accidentally bumps his hand?
   Is Tristan being mean here?
   Explain your point of view.

6. What does Tristan do next?
   Is this mean?
   Explain your point of view.

7. What does August compare himself to as the chapter ends?
   Do you understand what makes him say this?

8. Is August being bullied?
   Explain your point of view.

29. Costumes

Summary

August loves Halloween because he gets to dress up and wear a mask and be the same as everyone else.

August used to wear an astronaut helmet everywhere when he was younger, until he had to stop wearing it when he had his eye surgery. He could not find it after that.

This year he will dress as Boba Fett for Halloween. His mom has helped with his costume.

On the morning of Halloween, Via has a crying meltdown, so August's dad takes him to school. At the last minute, August does not feel like wearing his costume, and puts on his Bleeding Scream costume from last year.

Questions

1. Why does August like Halloween so much?

2. What positive does August see in everybody wearing masks all the time?
   What is he suggesting here?

3. Why did August stop wearing his astronaut helmet?

4. What do you notice about August's Halloween costume choices?

5. Describe August's costume this year.

6. What happens with Via on Halloween morning?
   Are her family concerned by her behaviour?

7. What does August do at the last minute?
   What reasons does he give for changing his mind?
   What, do you think, is his real reason for changing his mind?

30. The Bleeding Scream

Summary

August feels awesome walking through the corridors in his costume. He walks with his head up, wanting to be seen.

He walks into homeroom unnoticed and listens to Julian, dressed as Darth Sidious, talk to two mummies. They are talking about August's face.

One of the mummies says he would kill himself if he looked like August. Darth Sidious asks the mummy why he hangs around with him so much and the mummy shrugs, saying that August follows him around. August knows the mummy is Jack.

He leaves the room and walks downstairs crying, wanting to disappear.

Questions

1. Why is it awesome, walking through the corridors that morning?

2. Who has Julian dressed as?
   Explain his costume choice.

3. What conversation does August overhear between Darth Sidious and the mummies?

4. What does the second mummy say about August?
   How does this make you feel?

5. Who is the second mummy?
   How does this make you feel?

6. How is August feeling as the chapter ends?

7. What is the mood like at this point in the story?

31. Names

Summary

August cries in the bathroom and goes to the nurse's office, saying he feels sick.

His mom collects him and brings him home. He does not go trick-or-treating, or to school the following day. He does not want to go back to school again.

Questions

1. How does August spend first period?

2. Does his mother realise that he is not really ill?

3. How would you feel, if you were August?

4. How do you feel about what Jack said about August? Is there any excuse for saying these things?

5. What insight into August's life have you gained from reading up to this point?

6. Has reading Part One of this novel made you realise anything?
Explain your answer fully, including examples.

7. Why does the author begin this story from August's perspective, do you think?

8. Why does the author change perspective now, do you think?

Part Two - Via

32. A Tour of the Galaxy

Summary

Via compares August to the sun, at the centre of the universe, while she and her parents orbit around him.

She is used to not complaining to her parents or looking for attention because she realises the difficulties that August faces.

Now though, things are changing.

Questions

1. What does Via compare August to?
   Explain what she means here.

2. How have August's needs impacted on Via?

3. Is Via understanding about August?

4. Do you feel sorry for Via, reading this chapter?
   Explain your point of view.

5. What does the last paragraph in this chapter mean?

33. Before August

Summary

Via cannot remember a time before August.

There is a photo of her on her third birthday with all of her relatives, but she cannot remember it.

Just a little while after meeting August, she was all over him.

Questions

1. Describe Via's third birthday.

2. Why is she mentioning this party?

3. How did Via react when August was born? How must her parents have felt?

34. Seeing August

Summary

Via never used to see August as others do. She used to get mad when they stared at him.

Via went to stay with Grans for four weeks when she was eleven, when August was having his big jaw surgery. She loved the freedom of staying with Grans.

When she returned home, she had a flash of how other people view August, seeing the drool as he kissed her.

She never got to talk to Grans about this, as Grans died two months after Via stayed with her.

Via's mom crumpled to the floor sobbing when Grans died.

On her last day with Grans in Montauk, Grans told Via a secret, that she loved her more than anyone else in the world. This secret is something that Via held on to after Grans died.

Questions

1. How used Via react when people stared at August?

2. What was it like for Via, staying with Grans for four weeks?

3. What was it like for Via when she came home?

4. Was August happy to see her?
   How did she react to him?

5. Why didn't Via talk to Grans about how she sees August?

6. What does Via remember the most from the day Grans died?

7. What secret did Grans tell Via on her last day in Montauk?
   What is your response to this?

8. What are you learning about Via by reading this section?

9. Had you considered what life was like for Via while reading Part One?
   What is the author showing us here?

35. August Through the Peephole

Summary

Via describes August's facial features in detail.

He is often assumed to be a fire victim as his features look like they have been melted.

Since his jaw surgery, his tongue no longer hangs out of his mouth and he can eat. He has also learned to control the drool that used to run down his neck.

When he was a baby, the doctors did not think August would live.

Although he can hear now, the doctors think that August will need hearing aids.

Via wonders about what August knows and understands, and how he views himself. She wishes she could ask him about this stuff. He was easier to read before his surgeries.

Via says her family circle around August, when they should help him to grow up. She says the problem is they have convinced August that he is normal, when he is not.

Questions

1. Based on Via's description, describe August's appearance.

2. What makes people sometimes assume that August has been burned in a fire?

3. Why does August have scars around his mouth?

4. Why did August have a piece of his hip bone surgically implanted into his lower jaw?

5. What are "considered miracles" about August?

6. What do the doctors suspect about August's hearing?

7. What does Via wonder about August?

8. "I wish I could ask him stuff."
   What prevents Via from speaking openly with August?

9. Via says that August needs to grow up.
   Is she being harsh here, or is she right?
   Explain your point of view fully.

10. Via says that August thinks he is normal.
    Do you think this is the case?

11. Does Via sound frustrated to you?
    Can you explain how she is feeling?

36. High School

Summary

What Via loved most about middle school was being Olivia Pullman, separate to and different from home.

Everyone knew August at elementary school, but in middle school a lot of people did not. She does not want to be defined as the sister of someone with a birth defect.

The best thing about high school is that hardly anybody knows her.

She has been friends with Miranda and Ella since the first grade. They were all delighted to get into Faulkner High School.

Via cannot understand what is going on with her friends lately. High school is nothing like how she thought it would be.

Questions

1. What did Via love most about middle school?

2. Why did everyone know August when she was in elementary school?

3. What does Via not want to be defined as?
   What is your response to this?

4. What is the best thing about high school?

5. What did Miranda and Ella get without Via having to explain?

6. What can Via not understand lately?

7. Do you think that a lot of people find starting high school difficult?
   Give reasons for your answer.

37. Major Tom

Summary

Via's friend Miranda has always been sweet to August.

Via is surprised when Miranda does not call when she gets home from summer camp.

Via chats to her a bit online, but does not see her until the first day of school. She is shocked as Miranda has completely changed her image. Her hair is cut in a pink bob and she is wearing a tube top.

Miranda is distant with Via, treating her like a casual friend.

Via realises at lunch that Ella and Miranda have met up without her during the summer.

Questions

1. How has Miranda always treated August?

2. Why is Via surprised not to hear from Miranda?

3. Why is Via shocked to see Miranda on the first day of school?

4. How does Miranda treat Via on the first day of school?

5. What does Via realise at lunch?
   What is going on here?
   How would you feel, if you were Via?

6. Is Via surprised by how her friends are treating her?
   Are you surprised by their behaviour here?

38. After School

Summary

Via pretends that she does not need a lift home with Miranda, to avoid being in the car with this new version of her.

She lies to her mother when she gets home, pretending she is late because she had pizza with Miranda.

She goes to talk to August, wanting to know how his first day of school went. He is busy playing video games and says it was fine.

Questions

1. Why doesn't Via get a lift home with Miranda? Do you understand why she does this?

2. Why does Via yell at her mother, do you think?

3. Via goes straight to August's room when she gets home. What does this tell you about her relationship with her brother?

4. Do they have a good talk about the first day of school? Why/why not?

5. Is Via impressed by August's sarcasm, do you think?

39. The Padawan Bites the Dust

Summary

Via finds it difficult to explain why August cutting off his braid makes her mad.

She knew he was proud of it and cannot explain why she is so upset when he cuts it off.

Via's mom tries to talk to her about her day, but Via says she will talk to her later.

Her mom does not return though, as she is with August. Via has a good chat with her dad before she goes to bed.

Questions

1. Why, do you think, does Via get mad when August cuts off his braid?

2. Does Via's mother talk to her about her day?

3. Does Via talk to her father about her day?

4. Does Via have a good relationship with her parents, in your view?

40. An Apparition at the Door

Summary

One night, Via saw her mother standing outside August's room, watching him.

Her mother brought her back to bed that night, tucking her in and kissing her goodnight.

Via wonders how many nights her mother has watched over August, and whether she has ever watched over her the same way.

Questions

1. What did Via see one night when she woke up because she was thirsty?

2. What was her mother doing?

3. Explain what Via is asking in the final paragraph of this chapter.

41. Breakfast

Summary

Via wants to take the subway home after school. Her mom wants to call Miranda's mother to ask for a lift, but Via's dad says she is old enough to take the subway.

Via's mom realises that something is up. Via says she would have known about it if she had come back into her room, like she said she would.

Her mother says she is very sorry that she did not go back to her; she fell asleep in August's room.

When she hears that Miranda is being a jerk, her mom says that she will pick Via up, but Via's dad insists that she is old enough to take the subway.

Questions

1. Why does Via's dad say that she can take the subway home after school?
   What does this tell you about him?

2. What makes Via's mom realise that there is something going on with her?
   Is her mother perceptive here?

3. Do you feel sorry for Via's mom here?

4. Why does Via's dad insist that she can take the subway?
   What does this tell you about him?

5. What does Via's dad mean when he refers to "*War and Peace*"?

42. Genetics 101

Summary

Via's father's side of the family were Jews from Russia and Poland, while her mother's family are from Brazil.

She has looked at old family pictures, looking for a trace of August's face in theirs, but could find none.

After August's birth, her parents underwent genetic counseling. They both carry the gene that caused August's condition. Via also carries this gene.

Questions

1. What family history do you learn as this chapter begins?

2. Where did Via's parents meet?

3. Why does Via examine old photos of her family so closely?

4. Why did her parents undergo genetic counseling?

5. What caused August's condition?

6. What is the significance of the last line in this chapter? What is your response to this?

7. What do you know about genes and how we inherit traits from our parents?

43. The Punnett Square

Summary

Via considers the likelihood of her children inheriting August's condition.

She also considers the chances of August's children inheriting this condition.

Part of August's genetic make-up is not inherited, just incredibly bad luck.

Doctors have tried to explain the genetic lottery to her parents over the years, but there is still much they do not know.

They can try to foresee odds, but cannot guarantee them.

Via thinks of the countless babies who will not be born because of this, including her own.

Questions

1. What is the likelihood of Via passing on the defective gene to children of her own?

2. What is the likelihood of Via having a child that looks like August?

3. How do doctors explain the non-inherited part of August's genetic make-up?
   What do these terms mean?
   Are they easy to understand?

4. "Countless babies who'll never be born, like mine."
   What is Via telling us here?
   How has she come to this decision?
   Do you understand her decision?
   Do you think it was an easy or difficult decision for her to come to?
   Explain your point of view, referring to the text to support your answer.

44. Out with the Old

Summary

Olivia stops hanging around with Miranda and Ella.

At lunch she reads in the library, finishing *War and Peace*.

She starts hanging out with a smart girl called Eleanor she knew at PS22, and starts sitting at the smart-kids' table at lunch.

She has a crush on a boy called Justin who plays the violin.

She says hello to Miranda and Ella, but that is all.

Questions

1. What happened between Via and Miranda and Ella?

2. Who does Via start hanging out with?

3. What is the group of smart kids like?

4. Who is Justin?

5. How are things now with Miranda and Ella?

6. Are Olivia and August getting on well lately? Can you explain this?

45. October 31

Summary

This is a sad time of year for Olivia and her mother, as Grans died the night before Halloween, four years ago.

Olivia's mother spent two weeks working on August's Halloween costume.

On Halloween morning, Via starts crying over missing Grans. She stays home from school and cries with her mom, realising how important Grans was to her.

Her bonding time with her mother is interrupted when the nurse from August's school calls for him to be picked up.

Olivia's mother is very attentive to August.

Olivia understands that this is how her mother must be, as August is unwell.

Neither of them ask him why he did not wear the Boba Fett costume.

Questions

1. Why is this a sad time of year for Olivia?

2. Has Olivia's mother put a lot of work into August's costume, according to Olivia?

3. Why does she mention that her mother never made any of her costumes?
   Do you feel sorry for Olivia here, or should she get over this?

4. Why does Olivia start crying on Halloween morning?

5. In an earlier chapter, 'Costumes', August mentions Via crying, but does not know the cause.
   Does this tell you anything?

6. What does Olivia know about her mother's grief?

7. What stops Via from telling her mom about what is going on with Miranda and Ella?

8. Is Via jealous or understanding towards August in this chapter?

46. Trick or Treat

Summary

August does not feel up to trick-or-treating or the Halloween Parade. Via is surprised, as August is a trouper about medical issues.

She realises something is up and asks him if somebody said something. He tells her about overhearing the mean things Jack Will and the others said.

He says he hates school and gets angry, punching his pillow.

She lets him vent his anger and then convinces him to come to the Halloween Parade with her.

Questions

1. Olivia knows why August loves trick-or-treating. What does this tell you about her?

2. How does Via know that there is something up with August?

3. Why does August get so angry here?

4. How does Via comfort August? Does she make him feel better?

5. Why does August say that he hates school in this chapter? Would you feel the same way, in his position?

47. Time to Think

Summary

August's mother believes he is really sick and he stays off school on Friday. Olivia does not tell as she promised August she would not.

By Sunday, August is still adamant that he is quitting school. Via tells him he will have to tell their parents why he wants to quit.

She tells him that everyone hates school sometimes and he has to suck it up and go.

She also tells him that he should not let the kids he overheard get to him.

August asks Via if she just pretends to be friends with Miranda. Via asks what Miranda has to do with it. August says she called the other day, to talk to him.

Via says she will tell their parents about Jack Will if he stops going to school and Jack will probably have to apologise to him in front of everyone. Then August will be treated like he should be going to a school for kids with special needs.

August says he will go back.

He tells Via that Miranda said she misses her, which makes his sister happy.

Questions

1. What stops Olivia from telling their mother that August is not really sick?
   What is your response to this?

2. "...August was surprising me more and more."
   Why is Via surprised by her brother?

3. What arguments does Via come up with to convince August to go back to school?
   Is she successful?

4. Via tells August he can stop talking to the kids he overheard, or pretend to be friends with them.
   What would you do about this situation, if you were August?
   Would you talk to Jack Will about the cruel things he said? Why/why not?

5. What is your reaction to Miranda calling August on the telephone?

6. August eventually agrees to go back to school.
   What convinces him, do you think?

7. How does Via react to hearing that Miranda misses her?
   What is your response to this?

Part Three - Summer

48. Weird Kids

Summary

Other kids cannot understand why Summer has lunch with August.

She sat with him the first day because she felt sorry for him, on his own with everyone talking about him.

She does not think that sitting with August is a big deal.

Questions

1. How have other kids reacted to Summer sitting with August for lunch?

2. What made Summer sit with August the first time?

3. What nickname has Julian given August? What is your response to this?

4. What insight into Summer's character does her first chapter give you?

49. The Plague

Summary

Summer says that August's face takes some getting used to, and that he is not a neat eater.

She sits with him now because he is fun, not because she feels sorry for him.

Summer is not enjoying how kids are acting like they are too grown-up to play this year. She enjoys playing Four Square with August.

The Plague is a "game" where anyone who touches August has thirty seconds to wash their hands before catching the Plague.

Questions

1. What drawback is there to sitting with August?

2. Why does Summer keep sitting with him?

3. What is Summer not loving about this year?

4. What is the Plague?
   What is your response to this?

50. The Halloween Party

Summary

Summer is excited to be invited to Savanna's Halloween party. Savanna is the most popular girl in school.

Savanna tells her not to wear a costume. Summer is a little disappointed to be missing the Halloween Parade.

When she arrives, Savanna asks where her boyfriend is (meaning August) and comments on his not needing a mask.

All of the popular kids are at the party.

Henry wants to know why Summer hangs out with the Zombie kid so much.

Savanna says Summer would be a lot more popular if she did not hang out with August. She says that Julian likes Summer and that she must choose who she will hang out with.

Summer goes to the bathroom and phones her mom to collect her, leaving without seeing anyone.

Questions

1. Who is Savanna?

2. Savanna tells Summer not to wear a costume to her Halloween party.
   Does this surprise you?

3. What is the downside to going to Savanna's party?
   Would you still go?

4. How does Savanna greet Summer at the party?
   What is your response to this?

5. What does Henry want to know?

6. What choice does Savanna offer Summer?

7. Would you want to be part of Savanna's group of friends?
   Give reasons for your answer.

8. Why does Summer leave the party, do you think?
   Does she do the right thing here?

51. November

Summary

Summer tells Savanna she was sick and had to leave her party. She also says that she has a crush on someone other than Julian.

She knows something is up with August when he returns to school. He barely says anything and won't look at her at lunch.

She talks about their Egyptian assignments, trying to get him excited about them.

When Summer invites August to her house to work on their projects, he tells her that she does not have to be friends with him.

August believes that Mr. Tushman told Summer to be friends with him, but she convinces him that this is not the case.

He apologises and tells her what he overheard Jack Will saying about him. He makes her promise not to tell anyone.

Questions

1. What lies does Summer tell Savanna?
   Why does she do this?

2. Describe August's behaviour at lunch when he returns to school.
   Why is he acting like this around Summer?

3. What assignments did Summer and August get for Egyptian Museum Day?

4. Why is Summer a "little overexcited" about their Egyptian assignments?
   What does this tell you about her?

5. How does August react to being invited to Summer's house?
   How would you feel if you were her?

6. How does Summer react to August not trusting her?

7. Is Summer a good friend to August?

8. If you were Summer, would you talk to Jack about the hurtful things he said about August?
   Give reasons for your answer.

52. This Kid is Rated R

Summary

Despite Summer warning her, her mom is shocked by August's face when she meets him.

Summer tells her not to look so weirded-out and then her mom is really nice to August.

August sees a photo of Summer's dad and learns that he died a few years ago.

Summer thinks that when people die, they are born again, with another chance to live their lives right.

August likes the idea of being born again, with a completely different appearance.

Summer asks him what is wrong with his face, something she has not had the courage to do until now.

He explains that he has two syndromes that morphed and that it is a rare condition. He jokes that he is a medical wonder.

She smiles and says he is funny.

Questions

1. Why does Summer warn her mom about August's face?

2. Is her mother adequately prepared when she meets August?
   Does this tell you anything?

3. What do you learn about Summer's father in this chapter?

4. What happens to people when they die, according to August?

5. What happens to people when they die, according to Summer?

6. What do you think happens to people when they die?

7. What question does Summer have for August?
   What has stopped her from asking this question before now?

8. Does August mind these questions?
   Would you, if you were August?

53. The Egyptian Tomb

Summary

Over the next month, August and Summer spend a lot of time together after school, working on their exhibits.

On the day of the exhibition, the school gym is turned into a giant museum displaying the children's work.

Summer thinks that her and August's exhibits look great. They dress as mummies on the night and show their moms around by torchlight. It is a lot of fun.

Jack Will asks Summer if she knows why August is mad at him. He seems upset by it. She does not want to break her promise, so just tells Jack, "Bleeding Scream".

Questions

1. Are August and Summer getting along well?

2. What does the Egyptian Museum exhibit involve?

3. Describe August and Summer's exhibits.

4. Does this sound like a fun school event to you?

5. Has your school ever been involved in an event like this? If so, please give details.

6. How are the parents involved?

7. How do August and Summer dress for the exhibition?

8. Does Summer break her promise to August when she speaks with Jack Will?
   Would you have told Jack why August is mad at him?

9. Are you surprised that Jack wants to know why August is mad at him, considering what he said about him?

Part Four - Jack

54. The Call

Summary

Jack says Mr. Tushman called his mom in August to ask that he be a new kid's 'welcome buddy'. Mr. Tushman had heard good reports about Jack Will, so asked that he come and meet the boy before school started.

Jack's mom calls it flattering and sad. She tells Jack that there is something wrong with the boy's face.

Jack does not want to do it. He tells his mom that the new kid is deformed, knowing that it is August.

Questions

1. What is your response to the quote from *The Little Prince* that precedes this section?

2. Why might the author have chosen this quote for Jack?

3. Why does Mr. Tushman call Jack's mom in August?

4. Why was Jack selected by Mr. Tushman?

5. Does Jack want to be the new kid's 'welcome buddy'? What reason does he give for feeling this way? Would you do it, in Jack's position?

55. Carvel

Summary

Jack remembers seeing August for the first time when he was five or six and being scared by him.

Jack's babysitter, Veronica, left in a hurry as Jack and his little brother Jamie were staring. She was mad at them, and felt bad for rushing off.

Veronica told Jack that you do not need to intend to hurt someone, to hurt them.

Whenever Jack sees August after this, he tries to remember Veronica's words, but he finds it hard to act normal when he sees him.

Questions

1. Describe the first time Jack Will saw August.

2. Why was Jack's babysitter mad at him?

3. Were Jack and Jamie naughty here?

4. What made Veronica rush off?
   Why does she feel bad?

5. Jack says that it is hard to act normal when you see August.
   Is this a fair comment?

56. Why I Changed My Mind

Summary

Jack wants to know who else Mr. Tushman called. He is not impressed to hear that Julian and Charlotte are involved.

Jack tells his mom that she does not realise how bad August's face is.

His brother, Jamie, says that he had a nightmare about zombies after seeing August.

Jamie also says that when he saw August he screamed and ran away.

Jack's mom is disappointed that her sons are not more understanding and sympathetic.

Jack says he will do it. His mom is proud of him.

He feels that if nice kids like his brother can be mean to a kid like August, then he does not stand a chance. This is his reason for changing his mind.

Questions

1. What is Jack's opinion of Julian?

2. What is Jack's opinion of Charlotte?

3. What nightmare does Jamie have after seeing August?

4. Why is Jack's mom disappointed in her sons?
   Is she right to feel this way?

5. Jamie, Jack's little brother, does not understand the word "sympathetic".
   Without checking a dictionary, what do you understand this word to mean?

6. What makes Jack change his mind about helping August? What is your response to this?

57. Four Things

Summary

Jack says that you get used to August's face and that he is pretty funny, whispering things in class that crack Jack up.

He says that August is really smart and lets him cheat off him.

One time August lied to a teacher and said they had the same answers because they had worked together, to protect Jack from getting caught cheating.

Now that he knows him, Jack wants to be friends with August. August laughs at his jokes and Jack feels like he can tell August anything.

Questions

1. What four things does Jack tell us about August in this chapter?

2. How did August lie to protect Jack?

3. Why does Jack want to be friends with August?

4. Do you think that August would be a good friend to have?

58. Ex-Friends

Summary

Despite Summer's "Bleeding Scream" hint, Jack does not know why August is hardly speaking to him.

He has started ignoring August back, which is difficult, as they sit together in so many classes.

Other kids have noticed and asked Jack if they had a fight.

They only talk to one another about school stuff, and only if they absolutely have to.

Being apart from August, Jack gets to hang out with a lot more kids, as some kids avoided him when August was around.

Now, Jack can hang out with whoever he likes. The problem is, he does not like being with the popular group that much and liked spending his time with August.

He blames August for how messed up this is.

Questions

1. Has Summer's "Bleeding Scream" hint helped Jack figure out why August is barely talking to him?

2. How has Jack reacted to being ignored by August? How would you react, in his position?

3. Does August have many other friends, apart from Jack?

4. When do Jack and August speak to each other?

5. What is the positive side to not hanging out with August? What is your response to this?

6. Is Jack happier now that he is not spending time with August anymore?

7. Who is to blame for all this, according to Jack? Do you appreciate his point of view?

59. Snow

Summary

It snows before Thanksgiving break, and they get an extra day off school. Jack is happy not to have to see August every day.

Jack loves the quiet that snow brings to the world.

His dad takes him and his brother sledding. On the way home, Jack spots an old wooden sled that he takes home and fixes up.

He and his brother love sledding on '*Lightning*'.

When they return to school, he wants to tell August about the sled, but does not.

Questions

1. Why was Jack happy it snowed?

2. Is Jack upset by the situation with August, do you think? Do you feel sorry for Jack?

3. What does Jack like about snow?

4. Where does Jack's dad take him and his brother?

5. What does Jack find on the way home? How does he fix it up?

6. How does Jack feel, returning to school?

7. Why doesn't Jack tell August about his sled? Do you feel sorry for him here?

60. Fortune Favors the Bold

Summary

For Mr. Browne's December precept the class are to write about a time they were brave, and something good that happened to them because of this bravery.

Jack thinks that the bravest thing he has done is becoming friends with August. He does not write about this though, in case he has to read it out or his work is displayed.

Instead, he writes about being afraid of the ocean when he was little. He wonders what August writes about.

Questions

1. What are they supposed to write about for Mr. Browne's December precept?

2. What is the bravest thing Jack has ever done?

3. What stops Jack from writing about this?
   What is your response to this?

4. What does Jack write about instead?

5. Jack wonders what August will have chosen to write about.
   What would you write about here, if you were August?

61. Private School

Summary

Jack's parents are not wealthy. He shares a room with his brother and overhears their parents discussing money matters.

At recess, Julian, who is rich, moans about having to go to Paris for Christmas.

Jack says he hopes it snows so he can go sledding again. He is about to tell them about *Lightning*, when Miles mentions his new $800 sled.

Jack suggests they go sledding on Skeleton Hill, but Julian calls the hill junky.

Miles says he left his old, crappy sled at the bottom of Skeleton Hill. He is amazed that somebody took it away.

Jack walks away, not wanting anyone to know that he took the sled.

Questions

1. What do Jack's parents work as?

2. How do you know that Jack's family are not wealthy? Refer to specific details here.

3. What does Julian complain about at recess? What is your response to this?

4. What stops Jack from talking about *Lightning*?

5. Does Julian think that having a sled race down Skeleton Hill is a good idea?

6. What happened to Miles' old sled?

7. What does Julian suggest they do the next time it snows?

8. Why does Jack walk away from the others? How is he feeling?

9. Does this chapter tell you anything about wealth?

62. In Science

Summary

Jack is not a great student and does not really like school. He hates all the homework they get after being in class all day.

He hates science most of all.

When he was friends with August he did okay in science because August let him copy his notes. Now that they are no longer friends, he cannot ask to see his notes anymore.

Ms. Rubin mentions their science-fair projects, which makes Jack think of screaming. Suddenly, Summer's "bleeding scream" comment clicks with him.

He does not know why he said the mean things he said, he was just going along.

Realising August heard everything, Jack feels like puking.

Questions

1. Does Jack like school?

2. What does he hate most about school?

3. What class does Jack hate most?
   Why does he dislike this subject in particular?

4. Do you have a favourite or least favourite school subject?
   What makes you like/dislike this subject in particular?

5. How did being friends with August help in science class?

6. What is Jack's reaction to hearing about the fifth-grade science fair?

7. What does Jack suddenly realise?

8. How does Jack explain the mean things he said about August on Halloween?
   Do you understand why Jack acted this way?
   Can you excuse his behaviour here?

9. How does Jack feel, knowing that August overheard him?

10. What would you do now, if you were Jack?

11. Jack does not seem to like Julian, yet he cares what Julian thinks about him.
    Can you explain this?

63. Partners

Summary

Jack does not really hear what Ms. Rubin is saying. She begins assigning partners for the Science-fair projects, pairing Jack and August together.

After class, Julian tells Jack he should ask to switch partners. He even asks the teacher, but Jack says it is fine.

Julian follows Jack and tells him he does not have to be friends with the freak if he does not want to.

Jack punches Julian in the mouth.

Questions

1. Why doesn't Jack hear what Ms. Rubin is saying?

2. Who is Jack's Science-fair partner?
   Why is this a problem?

3. Why does Julian smirk at Jack?

4. What does Julian ask Ms. Rubin?
   Why does he do this, in your opinion?
   Does he really want to work with Jack, do you think?

5. Why does Jack punch Julian?
   What is your response to this?

64. Detention

Summary

Jack is in Mr. Tushman's office with his mom. They want to know why he hit Julian, but he is reluctant to tell them, thinking that it will make matters worse.

Mr. Tushman cannot understand why Jack will not explain himself.

Jack starts crying, but does not explain anything.

Mr. Tushman tells him to stay at home for the rest of the week. He asks him to think about what he has done, and to write a letter of explanation for him, and one of apology for Julian.

Questions

1. How does Mr. Tushman speak to Jack in his office?

2. How does Jack's mom speak to her son?

3. Why is Jack reluctant to explain why he hit Julian?

4. Why does Jack start crying?

5. What punishment is Jack given?
   Do you think this is fair?

6. How would you feel leaving Mr. Tushman's office, if you were Jack?

65. Season's Greetings

Summary

When Jack gets home there are holiday cards from Julian's and August's families in the mail.

Jack tells his mother he heard that Julian's mom photoshopped August's face out of the class picture.

He tells his mom why he hit Julian, and about Halloween and August being his ex-friend now.

Questions

1. What picture is on the holiday card from Julian's family?

2. What picture is on the holiday card from August's family?

3. What do these holiday cards draw our attention to?
   Explain your point of view.

4. What did Jack hear about Julian's mom?
   Do you think this could be true?

5. At the end of this chapter, Jack tells his mom everything.
   Do you think this will improve things?
   Explain your point of view.

66. Letters, Emails, Facebook, Texts

Summary

On December 18th, Jack sends a letter to Mr. Tushman, apologising for his behaviour. He does not give an explanation for hitting Julian.

He writes Julian a letter of apology on the same day.

Mr. Tushman sends a reply on December 26th. He suggests that while violence is not the answer, good friends are worth defending.
He tells Jack to keep up the good work.

Melissa Perper Albans, Julian's mother, emails Mr. Tushman on December 26th, supporting his decision to allow Jack to return to school after a two day suspension. She is certain that it will not happen again.

She suggests that asking Jack to befriend August was too much to expect of him, and that this may be the cause of his violent behaviour.

She goes on to question the decision to allow August into the school.

In his reply, Mr. Tushman states that August does not have any special needs and points out that he is an extremely good student.

He goes on to say that he did not think being kind to a new student would be a burden or hardship, but rather would teach about empathy, friendship and loyalty, virtues Jack Will already has in abundance.

Jack's father, John Will, emails Melissa, hoping to pay for Julian's dental bill. He assures her that Jack is happy to be August's friend.

Jack emails August to say sorry and to ask if they can be friends again.

Jack and August have a text conversation. August asks if Summer told Jack, and Jack explains about the hint she gave him.

August asks Jack why he punched Julian, guessing that it was about him.

He asks Jack if he would really kill himself if he were August and Jack assures him he would not. They are friends again.

Questions

1. Is Jack's letter from December 18 a good letter of explanation?
   Do you think Mr. Tushman will be satisfied with it?

2. Does Jack's letter to Julian on December 18 sound like a sincere apology?

3. What does Mr. Tushman say in his reply on December 26th?
   Is he an understanding man, do you think?

4. Why does Melissa Albans (Julian's mom) email Mr. Tushman on December 26th?

5. Is Melissa Albans angry that Jack hit Julian?

6. According to Julian's mom, what is the cause of Jack's violent behaviour?
   What is your response to this?

7. Why is Melissa a "little disturbed"?
   What is she really saying here?

8. On the basis of her email, what sort of person do you imagine Julian's mom to be?

9. How does Mr. Tushman respond to Melissa Albans' claims that August is not a suitable student for their school?

10. What is the tone of Mr. Tushman's email to Julian's mother?

11. If you were Mr. Tushman, how would you have replied to Melissa Albans' email?

12. What are the two main points in John Will's (Jack's dad's) email to Melissa?

13. Why does Jack email August?
How would you respond to this, if you were August?

14. What do they sort out in their text conversation?

15. Does this text conversation seem realistic to you?
Use examples to support the points that you make.

16. Why has the author decided to include letters, emails, Facebook and text messages in this chapter?
What does this add to the story?

67. Back from Winter Break

Summary

When Jack returns to school, Amos, Henry and Tristan all ignore him. He knows Julian is behind it.

Apart from the girls, both Maxes and August, nobody will talk to him. At lunch, Luca and Isaiah go and sit elsewhere.

Jack feels awful at the table by himself, so he skips lunch and goes to the library.

Questions

1. Why are things weird for Jack when he returns to school?
   What is going on here?
   What is your response to this?

2. What happens Jack at lunch?
   How would you feel, if you were him?

3. Why does Jack go to the library?

4. Can Jack fix this situation? How?

68. The War

Summary

Jack finds a note in his locker and goes to secretly meet Charlotte. She tells him that Julian had a huge party over winter break where he went around telling everyone that Jack punched him because he has emotional problems. He also said that Jack would have been expelled, if not for Julian's parents. He says the reason for Jack's behaviour is the pressure of being forced to be friends with August.

Charlotte's mom has heard that Julian's mother is pushing for the school to review August's application.

Julian says that being with August is bringing Jack down. He has convinced the boys to ignore Jack, maintaining this will be a wake-up call for him.

Apart from Savanna's group, the girls are not involved in ignoring Jack.

Charlotte will tell Jack if she hears anything else.

Questions

1. Why did Charlotte leave a note in Jack's locker?
   Why is she helping Jack?

2. Why is Charlotte so worried about being seen with Jack?

3. What information does Charlotte give him?

4. How does Jack respond to hearing what Julian has been saying about him?

5. According to what Charlotte has heard, what is Julian's mom trying to do?

6. How has Julian convinced the boys to stop being friends with Jack?
   Is this a convincing argument?
   Why are the boys going along with this, do you think?

7. Why is Charlotte still talking to Jack?

8. What view does Charlotte's mom have of Julian's mom?
   Does this surprise you?

9. Is Charlotte doing the right thing by passing this information on to Jack?

10. What would you do about this, if you were Jack?

69. Switching Tables

Summary

Jack tries sitting with Tristan, Nino and Pablo at lunch. They say "Hey", but do not return after their table is called.

The teacher tries to force them back to Jack's table, but he gets up and leaves.

Summer calls Jack over to sit with her and August.

Questions

1. What happens when Jack sits with Tristan, Nino and Pablo?

2. What does Mrs. G do?

3. Why does Jack walk away really fast?

4. Who calls Jack over?
   Does this surprise you?

70. Why I Didn't Sit With August the First Day of School

Summary

Jack remembers August being alone at lunch on his first day. Having spent all morning with him, Jack had purposely found a table far away from him, wanting a little normal time to chill with other kids.

He sits with Summer and August and tells them Julian has turned the whole grade against him.

Jack says it feels weird to have people pretending he does not exist. August smiles and welcomes Jack to his world.

Questions

1. Why didn't Jack sit with August on his first day?
   What is your response to this?

2. What did Jack think of Summer sitting with August?

3. Does August feel sorry for Jack here?
   Do you?

71. Sides

Summary

At lunch, Summer produces a list of who is on Jack's side, who is on Julian's side and who is neutral.

She tells Jack that she thinks that Charlotte likes him, but he says that he cannot ask her out now that everyone is acting like he has the Plague.

He apologises to August after he says this.

Summer says her mom thinks they are too young for dating. August says he agrees, which is a shame for all those babes throwing themselves at him. When Jack laughs at this, milk comes out his nose and the three of them crack up.

Questions

1. What does Summer produce at lunch?

2. What do you notice about the lists?

3. Where did Summer get this information?

4. Why does Summer ask Jack if he is going to ask Charlotte out?

5. What is Summer's mom's view of them dating? Do you agree with her?

6. What funny comment does August make?

7. Does Jack enjoy having lunch with Summer and August, do you think?

72. August's House

Summary

Jack goes to August's house to work on their science-fair project. He is nervous in case August has told his parents about the Halloween Incident, but August's mom is very nice to him.

Jack admires Daisy, August's dog and wants to play his Xbox 360, but August gets down to work. Jack is reluctant to choose a project, saying he sucks at science.

Via comes into the room. Jack realises immediately that August has told her about Halloween.

She tells August her friend is calling over. She wants August to meet him.

Questions

1. What makes Jack nervous about going to August's house? Would you be nervous too, if you were him?

2. What does Jack think of August's room?

3. Is Jack keen to get down to work?

4. What project does August want them to do? Does this sound interesting to you?

5. What does Jack realise when he meets Via?

6. Why does Via come into August's room?

73. The Boyfriend

Summary

Via introduces Justin to August and Jack. He is a little nervous.

Justin carries a fiddle case and August jokes that he should tell people it is a machine gun.

He tries to explain the type of music he plays, but the boys have never heard of it.

When he leaves with Via, the boys laugh at him.

Questions

1. Describe Justin.

2. What is in Justin's case?

3. Via says that Justin is in a zydeco band.
   Do you know what this is?
   Try to find out something that you do not already know about this type of music.

4. Does Justin make a good impression on August and Jack, do you think?
   Use examples to support your point of view.

Part Five - Justin

74. Olivia's Brother

Summary

Justin is taken aback when he meets August, even though Olivia told him about August's syndrome.

He tries to hide his surprise and tries not to focus on August's face.

He has been dating Olivia for two months and thinks she is great.

Olivia described August as having a craniofacial abnormality on their third date.

Justin lies to Olivia and says he is not shocked by August's face.

Olivia says a lot of kids never came back for a second playdate when she was little, once they had seen August.

She asks Justin if he is freaked out or scared by August and he tells her he is not. He thinks she believes him, or wants to at least.

Questions

1. Comment on the quotation that begins Justin's account.

2. What do you notice about the punctuation in this chapter?
   Why is it written like this?

3. How does Justin react to meeting August?

4. Was he expecting August to look like this?

5. What were Justin's first impressions of Olivia?

6. How did Olivia describe August's syndrome to Justin?

7. Why does Justin lie to Olivia and say he is not shocked by August's appearance?

8. Why does Olivia mention playdates to Justin?

9. Why does Olivia ask Justin if he is freaked out or scared?

10. How would you be feeling at the end of this chapter, if you were Justin?

11. How does Justin feel about Olivia?
    Use examples to support the points that you make.

75. Valentine's Day

Summary

Olivia and Justin exchange Valentine's gifts and make plans for him to meet her parents at dinner on Saturday.

Justin is very nervous about meeting her parents, but they are very friendly towards him and are interested in all he has to say. He is not used to the attention as he does not talk like this with his own parents.

They go to Olivia's after dinner for ice-cream. Daisy the dog has vomited in the hallway.

Olivia's dad tells Justin the story of how he bought Daisy from a homeless man, without even checking with Olivia's mom before he brought her home.

Justin likes Olivia's family. His family are not like them at all. His parents hate each other and could hardly wait for him to be old enough to look after himself. He has a half brother five years older than him, who barely knows he exists.

Questions

1. What gifts do Olivia and Justin exchange for Valentine's day?

2. How does Justin feel about meeting Olivia's parents?

3. What tics does Justin have?

4. How do Olivia's parents act towards Justin?
   Is he surprised by how they treat him?

5. Where do they go after dinner?

6. What has Daisy done?

7. How did Olivia's dad get Daisy?
   Is this a good story do you think? Why/why not?

8. What makes Justin like Olivia's family?

9. What are Justin's family like?
   How does this make you feel?

10. Why, do you think, have Justin's tics stopped by the time he goes home?

11. In what ways are Justin's family different to Olivia's family?
    What is the author showing us here?

76. Our Town

Summary

Justin gets the lead role in 'Our Town', the spring show.

Miranda gets the female lead.

Justin suspects that Olivia blew her audition on purpose.

Justin is apprehensive about how busy the next six weeks will be.

Questions

1. What role does Justin get in the spring show?

2. Who gets the female lead?

3. Why does Justin suspect that Olivia blew her audition on purpose?
   Why do you think, would she do this?

4. Why will Justin be busy for the next six weeks?
   Does this sound like fun to you?

5. Why did the drama teacher change the play they are putting on?

77. Ladybug

Summary

Olivia and Justin are sitting outside, practising his lines.

Justin is worried about memorising his lines.

Olivia catches a ladybug, which she sees as a good luck sign.

She tells Justin to make a wish on it, and he does. She tells him she made a wish too, but he has no idea what she wished for.

Questions

1. Describe the scene as this chapter begins.

2. What is Justin worried about?

3. How does Olivia interpret seeing the ladybug?

4. Why can't Justin guess what Olivia wished for? Can you guess her wish?

78. The Bus Stop

Summary

Olivia's mom, Auggie, Jack and Daisy come outside, interrupting Olivia and Justin kissing.

Olivia's mom asks Justin to walk Jack to the bus stop and wait with him.

Jack tells Justin he does not have to wait with him, but Justin says he will.

Jack goes to buy gum and Justin sees Julian, Miles and Henry trailing him, making loud throw-up noises.

Jack tells Justin about the war he is in with Julian. Justin says if he got the neutrals on his side it would even things up.

Jack says he is friends with someone who is not popular and Justin realises that this is about August.

On his way home, Justin sees Julian, Miles and Henry at the subway station. He makes himself look mean and warns them not to mess with Jack, tapping his fiddle case for effect.

Questions

1. What makes it awkward when Olivia's family appear?

2. What does Olivia's mom ask Justin to do?

3. What is Justin's view of Jack?

4. What happens when Jack goes into the grocery store?
   What is your response to this?

5. What is stopping Jack from getting the neutrals on his side?
   What is your response to this?

6. What advice does Justin give Jack?
   Is this good advice?

7. What does Justin do when he sees Julian, Henry and Miles later on?
   What is your response to this?

8. What made Justin do this, in your opinion?
   Do his actions here tell you anything about his character?

79. Rehearsal

Summary

Justin has lots of lines and long monologues to remember. Olivia came up with the idea of him having his fiddle on stage, which is helping him. He plays it a bit while he is talking.

He has got to know the kids in the show a lot better, especially Miranda.

One day Miranda asks Justin whether he has met Auggie. He is surprised to learn that she used to be good friends with Via, as Olivia had not told him anything about it.

She shows Justin a photo of August in his astronaut helmet and asks if he is okay with him.

Questions

1. What great idea does Olivia have to help Justin remember his lines?

2. What is Justin's view of Miranda?

3. What is Justin surprised to find out about Miranda?
   How would you feel, in his position?

4. What picture does Miranda show Justin?
   Why, do you think, does she show it to him?

5. What question does Miranda put to Justin?
   What does she mean by this?

6. This chapter ends with Miranda saying that the universe was not kind to Auggie Pullman.
   How would you respond to this comment, if you were Justin?

7. What are your feelings towards Miranda, at this point in the story?

80. Bird

Summary

Justin is really annoyed with Olivia for not saying that she used to be friends with Miranda. He thinks he looked like an idiot for not knowing.

She says that Miranda has changed and that she does not know her anymore, but Justin does not accept this excuse.

He sees she is crying and says he is not mad. Olivia says she does not care if he is mad.

He asks her what is the matter and the tears come fast.

She says she is an awful person. She has not told her parents about the show because she does not want August to come. She has enjoyed being in a new school where nobody knows about him. She feels terrible for being embarrassed of him.

Justin comforts Olivia.

Questions

1. Why is Justin annoyed with Olivia?
   Would you be annoyed too, if you were him?
   Do you think that Olivia should have told him about her friendship with Miranda?

2. What excuse does Olivia have?
   Is this a good excuse, in your view?

3. Why does Olivia start crying?
   Do you understand why she feels this way?

4. Do you think Olivia is an awful person for being embarrassed of her brother?

5. Why does Olivia remind Justin of a bird?

6. Does Justin care about Olivia, do you think?

7. Do Olivia and Justin have a good relationship?
   Use examples to support the points that you make.

8. What does Olivia not telling Justin about Miranda have to do with her getting upset?

81. Universe

Summary

Justin has trouble sleeping, thinking about his lines, schoolwork, Olivia and Auggie.

He thinks about the bad luck August had in getting his combination of syndromes.

Justin thinks that the universe is not all random though, because of the people in August's life who care so much about him.

Questions

1. Why can't Justin sleep?

2. Why does Justin say the universe is a giant lottery?

3. What makes Justin think that the universe "takes care of its most fragile creations"?
   What does this idea suggest about life?

Part Six - August

82. North Pole

Summary

August and Jack get As for The Spud Lamp at the science fair.

The projects are put on display and the students stand by their tables while the parents wander around and come over one by one.

August feels the eyes of all of the parents staring at him. This is why he dislikes school events involving parents.

He notices that his parents hang out with his friends' parents. His mom suggests that like seeks like.

Questions

1. Are you glad to be reading the story from August's point of view again? Why/why not?

2. How do Jack and August get on at the science fair?

3. How is the science fair set up?

4. What makes August compare himself to the North Pole? Do you feel sorry for August here?

5. Have there been many school events involving parents? What makes August dislike these events?

6. What does August notice about parents? Is this true, do you think?

83. The Auggie Doll

Summary

The war is at its worst in February. Practically no-one speaks to them and Julian leaves notes in their lockers. They also leave funny notes in Julian's locker.

Julian, Miles and Henry play tricks on Jack, like stealing his gym shorts and swiping his worksheet. They do not play tricks on August, for fear of getting in trouble for bullying him if they are caught.

The other kids begin to get sick of the war, and by March the majority of the boys are not buying into Julian anymore.

Julian spreads the rumour that Jack hired a hit man to get him and people laugh about him behind his back.

August thinks people have stopped playing the Plague game.

People even joke with him now. He jokes with Maya that the Uglydolls are based on him and she thinks he is really funny.

Questions

1. What made February the worst?

2. Why don't August and Jack report the notes?
   Would you, in their position?

3. Who is Beulah?
   Do you think this is a funny way to deal with the problem?

4. What tricks do Julian, Miles and Henry play on Jack?
   Why don't they do things like this to August?
   What does this tell you about them?

5. Why does August say that Jack is "good" about having these tricks played on him?
   Is it important to respond a certain way in situations like this?
   If you were Jack, what would you do about the situation with Julian?

6. Are Julian and his friends bullying Jack and August?

7. Why aren't the teachers aware of what is going on, do you think?

8. How does the war change in March?

9. What does Amos do?

10. What ridiculous rumour did Julian start spreading a few weeks ago?
    What effect does this have on their classmates?

11. What is really the cause of this rumour?

12. What makes August think that everyone has stopped playing the Plague game?

13. Why does August tell Maya that Uglydolls are based on him?
    What is her reaction to this?

14. How have things changed for August since starting school?

84. Lobot

Summary

August's hearing is worsening. He has not told anyone though, as he does not want to get hearing aids.

He fails the audiology test at his annual check-up and is sent to the ear doctor.

August groans when he sees his hearing aids as they look big, attached to a headband to keep them in place.

August says he will look like Lobot if he wears them, a *Star Wars* reference the ear doctor understands.

The ear doctor talks him through the parts of the hearing aids and slips them on. August complains they are uncomfortable and tears up when he looks at himself in the mirror.

Questions

1. Why doesn't August tell anyone that his hearing is getting worse?

2. How exactly, is his hearing affected?

3. How does August describe his ears?

4. Why doesn't August want to wear the hearing aids?

5. Why are the hearing aids attached to a headband?

6. Who does Auggie think he will look like if he wears the hearing aids?

7. How does August react to wearing the hearing aids?
   Why does he react this way?
   Do you feel sorry for August here?

85. Hearing Brightly

Summary

When the doctor turns August's hearing aids on, the ocean noise inside his head disappears and he hears 'brightly'.

He thought the kids at school would make a big deal about him wearing hearing aids, but no one does.

Questions

1. What is it like when the doctor turns on August's hearing aids?

2. Is he happy with his hearing aids?

3. How do the kids at school react to August's hearing aids?

86. Via's Secret

Summary

August's mom finds out about Via's school play and is very annoyed that Via kept it from her.

Via counters that she wants to be left alone, the way she has been for her whole life.

Questions

1. What does August's mom find out about?
   How does she react to this being kept from her?

2. How does Via retaliate?
   Is she being fair here, do you think?
   What is making her behave this way?

87. My Cave

Summary

At dinner, August asks if they are going to see Justin in a play. His mom tells him he would not be interested in the play, saying she will stay home with him while his dad goes.

Via yells at her mom, asking if she is being punished for being honest by her mother not going.

August accuses them both of lying, saying that Via does not want her new high school friends to know that her brother is a freak.

He goes to his room and hides under the covers. He is surprised that his mom does not come to check on him right away.

Questions

1. How are things by dinner?

2. How is Daisy?

3. What excuse does August's mom give him for why he is not going to Via's play?
   What do you think of this excuse?

4. What makes Via yell at her mother?

5. Why does August call Via and his mom liars?
   How would you feel if you were his mom or Via?
   How would you feel if you were August?

6. Why does August hide in a little cave on his bed?

7. What surprises him, as he waits under the covers?
   What is going on here, do you think?

88. Goodbye

Summary

Via tells August to come quick and say goodbye to Daisy as their mom is taking her to the emergency vet.

August insists that the vet will make Daisy better, but Via and his mom are not so optimistic.

They all cry as their mom takes Daisy away in a taxi.

Questions

1. Why has Via come into Auggie's room?

2. What state is Daisy in?

3. How does August react to Daisy being taken to the emergency vet?
   How would you feel in his position?

4. What makes this scene emotional?

89. Daisy's Toys

Summary

Justin comes over. Via and August have gathered all of Daisy's toys together. Via tells August about Daisy whimpering and panting. She bit their mother when she tried to pick her up.

Via says they should not have let Daisy get this bad. August is surprised by this, he did not realise how sick the dog was.

Via apologises to August for earlier. The fight does not matter much now.

August's parents return from the vet's, where Daisy has been put to sleep.

Later, August sees his father sitting on his bed, silently crying. His mother is in with Via, who is also in tears, so August puts himself to bed.

Questions

1. How was Daisy behaving?
   Does she sound ill to you?

2. Why is it significant that Daisy bit their mother?

3. Why hasn't August realised how sick Daisy is before now?

4. Are you surprised by how quickly Via and August make up after the fight at dinner?
   Give reasons for your answer.

5. What happened at the vet's?

6. Are the family very upset?
   Why do they feel this way?
   Are you surprised by their reaction?
   Do you feel sorry for them here?

90. Heaven

Summary

August wakes during the night and gets into his parents' bed. He apologises for the things he said earlier.

He asks his mother if Via is ashamed of him and whether Daisy is in heaven.

He wants to know if people look the same in heaven.

He cannot fall asleep, wondering how it will feel in heaven, when his face does not matter anymore.

Questions

1. What does August tell his mother when he gets into her bed?

2. What questions does he ask her?
   Does she give good answers, do you think?

3. Do his questions tell you anything about August or how he is feeling?

4. Why can't August fall asleep?
   What is your response to this?

91. Understudy

Summary

Via brings home three tickets for her show and the fight from dinner is not mentioned again.

It is August's first time in Via's new school. Because of his hearing aids, August cannot wear a baseball cap anymore. He wishes he could wear his old astronaut helmet.

They sit down and August's dad tells his mom that Miranda's father is getting remarried and has a baby on the way.

As soon as it starts, August knows he will like the play. It seems grown-up and he feels smart watching it.

To August's mother's surprise, it is Via, not Miranda, who comes onstage to play the role of Emily.

Questions

1. Via brings home three tickets for the school show. What has made her change her mind about this, do you think?

2. Why can't August wear a baseball cap anymore?

3. How does August feel about being in Via's new school?

4. What is an understudy?

5. What news does August's dad have about Miranda's family?
   Could this explain any of her recent behaviour, do you think?

6. Why is Miranda's mother not happy?
   How would you feel about this, if you were Miranda?

7. Why does August like the play right away?

8. Why is August's mom surprised when Miranda's character walks onstage?

92. The Ending

Summary

August thinks the play is amazing. Via actually cries at the end and the crowd give the performers a standing ovation.

His family go backstage and congratulate Via and Justin.

August is alone in the crowd and panics. He yells for Via and his mommy.

Someone picks him up from behind and hugs him tight. He sees it is Miranda and gives her a hug.

Questions

1. What is the play's ending like?

2. Is Via a good actress, do you think?

3. Is the performance a success?

4. Are August's parents pleased with the show?

5. Why wasn't Miranda in the play?

6. What happens when August finds himself alone in the crowd?

7. Who picks August up?
   How does he respond to this?

8. In what ways is August maturing and growing up?
   In what ways is August dependant on his family?
   Is he making good progress, do you think?

Part Seven - Miranda

93. Camp Lies

Summary

When Miranda's parents got divorced, her father was with someone else right away. Miranda thinks this is why they got divorced.

Miranda hardly ever sees her father now and her mother is distant and remote, never talking to her much.

Miranda did not want to go to camp this summer, wanting to stay and support her mother, but her mother insisted that she go.

Camp was awful. She did not know anyone. She began making up stuff about her family, including having a deformed brother.

She feels like a fake telling this lie, but also feels entitled to think of August as her brother as she has known him for so long.

These lies made her very popular at camp.

When she gets home, she does not call Via. Ella is an easier friend to have, as she never asks about things and is not serious, like Via.

Questions

1. Why did her parents get divorced, according to Miranda?

2. What is Miranda's relationship with her father like after the divorce?

3. What is Miranda's relationship with her mother like? How did this change after the divorce?

4. Why didn't Miranda want to go to camp the summer before ninth grade?

5. What made camp awful?

6. Why did Miranda say that she has a little brother who is deformed?
What is your reaction to her lie?

7. "…I've kind of earned the right to think of him as my brother."
Is Miranda entitled to think of August as her brother? Explain your view.

8. How do the campers and counselors react to Miranda's fictions?

9. Why doesn't Miranda call Via when she gets home from camp?

10. Why is Ella the friend she calls right away?
What does this tell you about Miranda?

11. What are your impressions of Miranda, after reading this chapter?

94. School

Summary

Miranda finds seeing Via at school awkward.

She thinks that Via disapproves of her new look and new friends.

Miranda and Ella badmouth Via and ice her out.

They have changed, while Via has not.

Miranda sees Via with Justin and is surprised to realise that she has a boyfriend.

When she sees Via's name on the theatre elective list, Miranda signs up.

When photocopying for Mr. Davenport, the drama teacher, Miranda saw he had chosen *The Elephant Man* for the spring production. This play is about a terribly deformed man.

Miranda told the teacher that he could not stage this play as her brother has a deformed face and her parents would have an issue with it. This is how they ended up doing *Our Town*.

Miranda went for the Emily Gibbs role because she knew that Via was going for it. She did not expect to get the role over Via though.

Questions

1. What is it like for Miranda when she sees Via at school?

2. Is Miranda treating Via fairly?

3. Why is Miranda behaving this way towards Via?

4. How does Miranda discover that Via has a boyfriend?
   What is your response to this?

5. What is Zack, Miranda's boyfriend, like?

6. What made Miranda sign up for the theatre elective?

7. What play was Mr. Davenport planning to stage?

8. Why does Miranda make Mr. Davenport change the play?
   What reason does she give?
   What is your response to this?
   Is Miranda doing this for Via?

9. Is Mr. Davenport happy to change the play?

10. Why does Miranda go for the role of Emily Gibbs?
    Does this tell you anything about Miranda's relationship with Via?

11. Describe and analyse Miranda's friendship with Via, based on what you learn in this chapter.

12. Do you think that the chosen play should have been switched like this?
Give reasons for your answer.

95. What I Miss Most

Summary

Miranda misses Via's family. She called their house to say hello to Auggie. She is shocked to hear that he goes to a regular school now.

She tells him she misses him and that he can call her anytime. Miranda asks August to tell Via that she misses her.

Questions

1. What does Miranda miss most about Via's friendship? Do you feel sorry for her here?

2. Was Miranda a good friend to Via when she was younger?

3. How does Miranda treat Auggie?

4. Why does Miranda call Via's house?

5. What is Miranda's response to hearing that August goes to a regular school now?

6. Miranda tells August that she misses Via. Do you feel sorry for her? What should she do about this?

7. What does Miranda's perspective add to the story?

96. Extraordinary, but No One There to See

Summary

Neither of Miranda's parents are free to come to the play. Zack is playing a volleyball match the same night, so all of her friends go to that.

Miranda knows she will give an extraordinary performance, but there is no one close to her there to see it.

Miranda sees Via's family in the audience and surprises herself by telling Davenport that she is sick and cannot go on.

Mr. Davenport is very annoyed. He sends for Olivia to fill in for Miranda.

As she gets into costume, Olivia asks Miranda why she is doing this, but she does not get a chance to answer. Miranda does not know what her answer would have been.

Questions

1. Why can't Miranda's parents come to the play?

2. Why can't Zack come to see it?

3. Why don't any of Miranda's friends come?
   How does this make you feel?

4. What does Miranda realise in her third or fourth rehearsal?

5. "I was going to be extraordinary, but there would be no one there to see."
   How does this line make you feel?

6. What differences does Miranda notice in August when she sees him?

7. Why, do you think, does Miranda tell Mr. Davenport that she cannot go on tonight?
   What do you think of this?

8. How does Mr. Davenport react to Miranda letting him down?
   How does he treat her here?
   Would you act the same way, in his position?

9. What does Olivia think of Miranda's sickness?

10. At the end of the chapter, Miranda says she does not know why she did this.
In your opinion, why did she do this?
What is your response to this?

97. The Performance

Summary

Miranda watches the play from the wings, next to a very nervous Davenport.

She thinks Justin is amazing and thinks that Olivia is awesome in the final scene.

When the audience rise to their feet at the curtain call, Miranda feels some regret, until she sees how happy Olivia's family are backstage.

She notices August looking lost in the crowd and goes to him.

Questions

1. What does Miranda think of the play?

2. How does Davenport feel, watching the play?

3. When does Miranda regret backing out of the play?

4. What makes her feel better about her decision?

5. Has your view of Miranda been changed by this section from her perspective?
Include examples to support the points that you make.

98. After the Show

Summary

Miranda is very happy to see August after so long.

She tells Isabel (August's mom) that not being in the play is not a big deal as her mom had to work and there will be two more shows.

Isabel invites Miranda to join them for a celebratory dinner. Miranda begins to turn her down, until Via puts her arm around her and insists that she join them.

Questions

1. Has Miranda missed August?

2. How do Olivia's family treat Miranda when they meet her?

3. Why does Miranda begin to turn down the invitation to dinner?

4. What makes her change her mind?

5. What is the mood like as this chapter ends?

6. Do you think that Miranda and Olivia will become good friends again?
   Give reasons for your answer.

Part Eight - August

99. The Fifth Grade Nature Retreat

Summary

Each year, the fifth graders go to a nature reserve and stay in cabins for two nights.

Everyone is excited about it, but August is nervous as he has never slept away from home before.

When he was eight he wanted to sleep over at his friend Christopher's, but he started crying at bedtime and his dad drove back to get him.

Questions

1. What does the fifth grade nature retreat involve?

2. Is August excited about it?

3. Would you be excited about a trip like this?
   Give reasons for your answer.

4. Why has August never been on a sleepover?

5. What happened when August slept over at Christopher's when he was eight?
   Does this sound like a "disaster" to you?

6. Do August's parents make a lot of allowances for him?
   Do they make too many?
   Explain your answer fully.

100. Known For

Summary

August gets a new rolling duffel bag for the nature retreat. His old one was a Star Wars one and he does not want to be known for that.

He says that you have to be careful about what you are known for in middle school.

He knows what he is really known for, but he cannot do anything about that, whereas he can do something about a *Star Wars* duffel bag.

Questions

1. Why does August get a new rolling duffel bag?

2. What are Reid, Amos, Charlotte and Ximena known for?

3. Why do you have to be careful about what you are known for, according to August?
   Do you agree with August on this?

4. Do you think that August is less concerned with his appearance than when he started school?
   Use examples to support the points you make.

101. Packing

Summary

As August and his mom pack his duffel bag, he worries that he won't be able to sleep or will have a nightmare on the trip.

He decides to bring Baboo, a stuffed bear, and hide him in his bag.

His mom notices that he has taken down his *Empire Strikes Back* poster.

She reminds him to wear bug spray and sunscreen, and not to get his hearing aids wet.

She comments on how much August has grown up this year.

He has to go to bed as he has a six a.m. start the next day. August tells his mom she does not need to put him to bed, which impresses her.

August reads *The Lion, the Witch and the Wardrobe* until he falls asleep.

Questions

1. What concerns does August have as he packs his bag?

2. Who is Baboo?
   Is bringing Baboo a good idea?

3. Does August's mom do a good job of reassuring him?
   Give reasons for your answer.

4. What is significant about August taking down his *Empire Strikes Back* poster?

5. What different things does August's mom remind him about for the trip?

6. Do you think August's mom is anxious about him going on this overnight trip?
   Give reasons for your answer.

7. Why doesn't August want to go to bed?
   Have you ever had to go to bed early to be up for a trip or holiday?
   Could you get to sleep easily?

8. What impresses August's mom at bedtime?
   What does this tell you about August?

9. What book is August reading?
   Do you know anything about this story?
   Is it worth reading?

10. Does August have a good relationship with his mom? Include examples to support the points that you make.

102. Daybreak

Summary

August has a dream where he wakes up and sees Daisy by his bed. It fills him with nice feelings to see her.

He hears birds, garbage trucks and his mom's alarm as it gets light.

He takes Baboo out of his bag and leaves him behind with a note for his mom.

Questions

1. What does August see by his bed?
   How does this make you feel?

2. What does August see and hear as he wakes up?

3. What does August do with Baboo?
   Is this a good idea, do you think?

4. How will August's mom feel when she reads his note, do you think?

103. Day One

Summary

Everyone is in a good mood on the bus trip.

August is happy to hear that Julian has not come on the nature retreat excursion.

August gets a top bunk in his cabin.

They have lunch and go on a two-hour guided nature hike. It starts raining, so they spend the afternoon in the rec room and have a campfire cookout at dinnertime.

August loves hanging out by the campfire after dark.

He is so tired when he gets back to the cabin that he falls asleep straight away.

Questions

1. What is the bus trip like?

2. How does August feel when he hears that Julian is not going on the trip?

3. What do you think of Julian's reason for not going?

4. What do they do on their first day at the nature reserve?

5. What is the hike like?

6. What do they do in the rec room?

7. Describe the campfire cookout.

8. Is August having a good time?

9. Does this sound like a fun trip to you? Include examples to support your answer.

104. The Fairgrounds

Summary

The next day they go horseback riding and tree rappelling. After dinner they will go to the fairgrounds for an outdoor movie.

August writes his family a letter.

He admires the sunset when they reach the fairgrounds.

They are the first school to arrive, so they run around and spread out their sleeping bags in good viewing spots, before loading up on snacks.

They play pictionary as darkness falls and the other school buses arrive.

When the big lights go on, everyone claps and cheers.

Questions

1. How do they spend the next morning and afternoon? Does this sound like fun to you?

2. What is the plan for after dinner?

3. Why does August write a letter to his family?

4. How does August describe the sunset?

5. What benefit is there in being the first school to arrive?

6. Where will they watch the movie from?

7. What snacks are available?

8. What "big gossip" goes around?

9. What do they do as they wait for the movie?

10. - What do the lights make August think of?

11. Does this sound like a fun evening to you?

105. Be Kind to Nature

Summary

A voice comes over the speakers, welcoming the various schools, to much cheering.

It asks them to respect nature and clean up after themselves. It asks them to remain in the fairgrounds and be courteous to fellow students who are watching the movie. Students are also asked to stay with their school groups on the way back to the buses so that nobody gets lost.

The movie that is playing is *The Sound of Music*. August claps, as it is Via's favourite, but a bunch of kids from another school boo, hiss and laugh.

Questions

1. What is the atmosphere like before the movie begins?

2. What important announcement is made over the speakers?

3. What movie is showing?

4. Is August happy with this choice?
   How do some other kids react to the movie selection?
   Would you watch this movie?

5. Do you think that the movie selection is important on a night like this, or does it not matter very much? Explain your point of view fully.

106. The Woods are Alive

Summary

Jack has to pee, so he and August leave the movie. The queue for the toilets is huge, so Jack decides to find a tree instead.

It is difficult to see in the woods without a flashlight. They pass Henry, Miles and Amos, walking towards them.

The woods are loud with strange sounds.

August also pees. The boys notice the smell of firecrackers.

Questions

1. Why do August and Jack leave the movie?

2. Why does Jack decide to find a tree?

3. Why is it difficult to see in the woods?

4. Who do they pass in the woods?

5. What is it like in the woods, at this time?

6. What smell do the boys notice?

107. Alien

Summary

Heading back to the movie, they run into six kids who smell of cigarettes and firecrackers.

One of the girls starts screaming when she sees August's face and the others laugh and cover their eyes.

Jack tries to leave, but the boy with the flashlight cuts them off.

They call August 'Gollum' and laugh at him.

The boys try again to walk away, but are cut off by the kid named Eddie.

The kids call August names (alien and orc).

Jack tells Eddie, the ringleader, to leave August alone. Eddie is aggressive, pushing Jack and knocking him down.

When August speaks, Eddie calls him Freddy Krueger and an ugly freak.

Amos arrives with Miles and Henry. He tells Eddie to leave them alone. Amos tells August and Jack that Mr. Tushman is waiting for them, which

August knows is a lie.

As August walks over to Amos, Eddie grabs his hood and yanks him backwards. August falls on the ground and Amos rams into Eddie.

Everything is crazy after this. People pull August in different directions and his sweatshirt rips. There is shouting, cursing, footsteps and voices behind them as they run.

Questions

1. What do the kids they meet smell of?

2. How do these kids react to seeing August?
   What is your response to this?
   What would you do here if you were August and Jack?

3. When they try to walk away, the boy with the flashlight 'cuts them off'.
   What does this mean?
   How would you feel if you were August or Jack?

4. What names do the kids call August?
   What is your response to this?

5. What does Jack say and do to reason with Eddie?
   Does this work?

6. Does August reason with Eddie?

7. Who arrives on the scene?
   What do they do?
   Are you surprised by this?
   Explain your response here.

8. Why does Amos say that Mr. Tushman is looking for them?

9. What does Eddie do to August as he walks over to Amos?
   What is your response to this?

10. What does Amos do to Eddie?
    What is your response to this?

11. August says things "got really crazy".
    Explain what happens next.
    How would you feel here if you were August?

12. What makes this a tense and exciting moment in the story?

108. Voices in the Dark

Summary

After running for ages, they stop, hoping they have lost the others. They listen for footsteps, but hear none. They are all out of breath.

Henry, Miles and Amos had seen the other kids, that is how they knew to go back after August and Jack.

The boys laugh about the fight and their get-away.

They try to figure out where they are.

Jack thanks the others for coming back for them and they each high-five him, and then August.

They are impressed with the way August stood his ground against the other kids.

August's sweatshirt is torn and his elbow is bleeding. He tries not to cry.

Jack sees that August's hearing aids are gone and August begins sobbing. The other boys are nice to him.

Questions

1. Who was pulling August along as they ran?
   Why is this significant?

2. Why do they go super quiet?
   How would you be feeling, if you were there?

3. What made Henry, Miles and Amos come back for Jack and August?

4. How are the boys feeling?

5. Where are they?

6. Miles, Henry and Amos all high-five Jack and August. How does this make you feel?

7. How has August impressed the other boys?

8. What state is August's sweatshirt in?

9. What injury does August have?

10. Why does August start to cry?

11. How do the other boys react to August's tears?
    What is significant about this?

12. What has changed for August in this chapter?
    What is your response to this?

109. The Emperor's Guard

Summary

They backtrack and look for August's hearing aids, but it is too dark to see anything, so they head back to the movie screen.

August does not want to report the other kids. Amos tells him not to walk around alone. His classmates surround August as they walk through the crowds of kids.

Questions

1. Why can't they find August's hearing aids?

2. August does not want to report the other kids. Explain his decision here.
   Would you report them, if you were August?

3. What advice does Amos give August?
   What makes him say this?

4. Why is this chapter called 'The Emperor's Guard'?
   What does the boys' behaviour here tell you?

110. Sleep

Summary

August stops reading just before two a.m. He cannot sleep, afraid of how dark it is.

He is surprised that such a bad night for him was ordinary for other people.

When they rejoined their classmates at the movie, each of the boys sat with their friends as before, but something had changed.

Amos, Miles and Henry told their group about what happened and news of it spread.

The girls ask August if he is okay and the boys talk about getting revenge on the seventh-grade jerks.

The teachers hear about what happened. Mr. Tushman takes August to the first-aid office. He tries to get a description of the troublemakers from the boys.

August says he cannot remember their faces, which is a lie. Thinking of the looks of horror and hatred on their faces is what is keeping him awake.

Questions

1. Where is August and what is he doing?

2. Why can't August sleep?

3. What surprises August when he thinks about the day's events?

4. "Something had changed."
   Explain what August means here.

5. In the long term, do you think the night's events are a positive or a negative thing for August and Jack?
   Fully explain your point of view.

6. Are you surprised that the teachers find out about what happened?
   How do they respond?

7. Why does August say that he can't remember the faces of the kids in the woods, do you think?

8. What is really keeping August awake?
   How must he be feeling?

111. Aftermath

Summary

Mr. Tushman has called August's mom. He told her that there was a situation, but that August is fine.

Broarwood (Eddie's school) will reimburse August for the cost of his hearing aids, as they could not be found.

His mom hugs him tightly when he gets off the bus, but does not ask him anything.

A lot of the other kids nod hello or pat his back as he walks by.

Mr. Tushman hugs him as he starts to walk away.

Questions

1. Who will replace August's hearing aids?
   Does this surprise you?

2. How does August's mom react when she sees him?
   How must she be feeling?

3. Why, do you think, does Mr. Tushman hug August before he leaves?

112. Home

Summary

August and his mom do not talk much on the walk home. She gives him a huge hug and kisses him when they get in.

He tells her that the trip was great, apart from the last night. His mom says he cannot let the awful part take away from his enjoyment of the trip.

August asks if Mr. Tushman told them about his hearing aids. He thinks his dad might be mad about him losing them as they are so expensive.

August chats about the fight with his mom, but asks that he tell her the whole story later, when his dad and Via get home. He does not want to have to retell it.

August finishes eating. He asks his mom if he is always going to have to worry about jerks like that, even when he grows up.

She answers that there will always be jerks, but says she believes there are more good people than bad people in the world.

August's dad and Via come home. They hug and kiss August and give him a new puppy.

Questions

1. What does August's mom do as soon as they get home?

2. Where are Via and August's dad?

3. Did August have a good time on the trip?

4. Why is August concerned about the hearing aids?

5. What makes August laugh at his mom?

6. Why doesn't August tell his mom all about what happened with the seventh graders?

7. 'Am I always going to have to worry about jerks like that?'
   How does August's question make you feel?
   What answer would you give him?

8. How does August's mom answer his question?
   What does her answer tell you about her outlook and personality?
   Do you agree with her outlook?
   Give reasons for you answer.

9. Why did August's dad leave work early?

10. How do his dad and sister greet him?

11. What present have they brought August?

12. Do August's family communicate and get along well together?
Use examples to support your point of view.

113. Bear

Summary

They name the puppy Bear. August and Via stay home from school the next day to play with him.

August enjoys hanging out with Via for the day, as they have not done it often since he started school.

Questions

1. Why do they name the puppy Bear?

2. Why does August stay home from school the next day? Would you be allowed to stay home from school like this? Why is August allowed to?

3. Why is hanging out with Via fun?

4. Why haven't August and Via hung out much lately?

114. The Shift

Summary

A big shift has occurred in school. August is no longer known for his face, but for the episode with the seventh graders.

The story has been exaggerated and added to. However, August getting picked on because of his face, Jack defending him, and Amos, Miles and Henry protecting him, are the same in each version of the story.

The kids at school view August differently now and accept him.

Amos has become really popular, while Julian is out of the loop as he missed the trip. Julian still does not speak to August or Jack, but he is the only one like this now.

Questions

1. "...there was a big shift in the way things were."
   What does this line mean?

2. What "big shift" has occurred?

3. How has the story of what happened with the seventh graders changed?
   Does this often happen when stories are retold, do you think?

4. Whose version of the story is best?
   What makes this one the best?

5. What two things always stay the same in the re-telling of the story?
   Why is this significant?

6. How has the incident with the seventh graders affected Amos' popularity?

7. How has this incident affected Julian?

8. How does Julian treat August and Jack these days?
   Can you explain his behaviour?

115. Ducks

Summary

Mr. Tushman calls August into his office.

The mangled remains of August's hearing aids were found in Eddie's locker. His school want to know if August will press charges.

August is not keen on this idea, but Mr. Tushman thinks a trip to juvie court might teach Eddie a lesson.

Mr. Tushman invites August to sit down and chats with him about how the school year has been for him.

Mr. Tushman says that Julian will not be back to Beecher Prep next year.

August's drawing of himself as a duck is hanging on Mr. Tushman's wall. He asks August why he chose to depict himself as a duck. He laughs when he hears it is because August thinks he looks like a duck. He had been expecting a more symbolic meaning.

Mr. Tushman tells August it has been a pleasure to have him at Beecher Prep.

Questions

1. Why does Mr. Tushman call August into his office?

2. What was found in Edward's locker?

3. What does Edward's school want to know?
   What would you do here, if you were August?

4. What does Mr. Tushman want August to do, do you think?

5. What does Mr. Tushman chat with August about?

6. How does Mr. Tushman surprise August?

7. What news does Mr. Tushman have about Julian?
   What is your response to this?

8. What is hanging on Mr. Tushman's wall?

9. What makes Mr. Tushman laugh?

10. What is the mood like as this chapter ends?

11. Is Mr. Tushman a good middle-school director in your opinion?
    Use examples to support your ideas.
    Is he a kind man?
    Explain your point of view.

116. The Last Precept

Summary

Mr. Browne's June Precept is 'Just follow the day and reach for the sun!'

His message reminds students to send him their own personal precepts over the summer.

Questions

1. What is Mr. Browne's June Precept?

2. What does this mean?

3. What does Mr. Browne ask his students to do over the summer?

117. The Drop Off

Summary

August's dad drives him to his graduation ceremony as he is all dressed up and wearing new shoes.

They arrive early, so sit in the car listening to music. They talk about how smart and grown-up August looks.

His dad says he used to hate the astronaut helmet August wore so much, that he threw it out.

August is mad when he hears this. His dad says he could not stand seeing the helmet covering August's face. He did not think it was good for him.

August asks if his mom knew. His dad says of course not, and swears August to secrecy. August jokes about what he will need for his silence to be bought.

They sing and laugh together and August forgives his dad.

Jack arrives. Before his dad drives away, August asks that his family not kiss him a lot after graduation, as it is embarrassing.

Questions

1. Why do they drive to the graduation ceremony?

2. How do they pass the time while they wait?

3. What do they talk about as they wait?
   How is August feeling?
   How is August's dad feeling?

4. What really happened to August's astronaut helmet?
   How does August react to this news?
   How would you feel, if you were him?

5. Did August's dad do the right thing here, do you think?
   Do you understand why he acted as he did?

6. Does August's mom know what happened to the astronaut helmet?

7. How is the matter of the astronaut helmet resolved?
   What insight does this give you into their relationship?

8. What request does August make of his dad as he leaves?
   What does this tell you about August?
   What does it reveal about his family?

118. Take Your Seats Everyone

Summary

The auditorium has sparkly chandeliers, red velvet walls and rows of cushioned seats.

August and Jack go to the fifth-grade staging area where Ms. Rubin organises the kids alphabetically. They do not listen to her though; Jack and August sword-fight with their programs.

Summer arrives and August tells her she looks awesome. Jack says she looks okay, and August realises that Jack has a crush on her.

Jack looks at the program and remarks that they will be there all day.

They expect Charlotte and Ximena to win all of the awards, like they do every year.

As they take their seats, Jack wonders when Summer got so hot. He sits in the wrong place and cracks August up with the look on his face when he gets up to move.

Questions

1. What is it like inside the auditorium?

2. How are they organised in the staging area?

3. What do August and Jack do while Ms. Rubin is speaking? Can you explain their behaviour here?

4. What makes August realise that Jack has a crush on Summer?

5. What is Jack's reaction when he looks at the program?

6. What is the awards presentation?

7. Who do they expect to win all of the awards?

8. How does Jack crack August up?

9. What is the mood like as this chapter ends?

119. A Simple Thing

Summary

Mr. Tushman thanks everyone attending and begins his graduation address.

He says he cannot use the same speech for his fifth and sixth grade graduation as for the seventh and eighth grade one, because the younger grades are at an age of transition and possibilities.

Mr. Tushman says when they measure how much they have grown this year, they should think about how they have spent their time, and whom they have touched.

He reads a line from a book saying that we should be kinder than necessary and talks about what a good idea this is.

He reads another excerpt about kindness and impresses on his students that anything is possible. If everyone is a little kinder, the world will be a better place.

Questions

1. Why doesn't Mr. Tushman reuse his graduation speech each year?

2. According to Mr. Tushman, what is significant about the age the fifth and sixth graders are at?
   Do you agree with him?

3. Why are they all gathered there, according to Mr. Tushman?

4. How can they measure how much they have grown this year?
   Do you agree with what Mr. Tushman says here?
   Give reasons for your answer.

5. What line does Mr. Tushman read from *The Little White Bird*?
   Do you think this is a good rule?
   Give reasons for your answer.

6. Why does Mr. Tushman love this line?

7. What is the piece from *Under the Eye of the Clock* about?

8. What does Mr. Tushman want to impart to the children?

9. Do you think this is a good graduation speech?
   Give reasons for your answer.

120. Awards

Summary

Ms. Rubin reads the names of the students on the High Honor Roll. August stands when his name is called and bows to the audience.

Ximena, Charlotte, Amos and Summer each win medals for academic excellence.

Mr. Tushman introduces the Henry Ward Beecher medal, an award to honour notable or exemplary students.

He speaks again about kindness and gets choked up, something that catches August's attention.

According to Henry Ward Beecher, greatness is about carrying up the most hearts.

Mr. Tushman gets choked up again before awarding this honour to August.

Questions

1. Does August enjoy the graduation speeches?

2. How are the students on the High Honor Roll acknowledged?

3. Who wins the medals for academic excellence?

4. What is the final award and what is it given for?

5. What do 'notable' and 'exemplary' mean?

6. What makes August focus on what Mr. Tushman is saying?

7. What four qualities define us as human beings, according to Mr. Tushman?
   Do you agree with him?
   Explain your view.

8. What is 'Greatness', according to Beecher?

9. Are you surprised that August wins this award?
   Does he deserve it? Why/why not?

10. How would you feel, if you were August?

11. Why, do you think, does Mr. Tushman get so choked up when presenting this award?

121. Floating

Summary

The kids clap and cheer for August. He beams as he walks towards the stage.

As he climbs the steps, the whole audience gets to their feet, clapping and whooping for him.

He knows he is getting this award for being the person whose life other people cannot imagine.

To him, he is an ordinary kid.

He is happy to have the medal. He sees getting through the fifth grade as an achievement.

Questions

1. What is the reaction to August winning this award?

2. How does August feel about winning this award?

3. What happens as August walks up the steps to the stage?

4. Why is he getting this award, in August's view?

5. How does August see himself?

6. What is the mood like in this chapter?

7. Is this a very emotional chapter, do you think? Give reasons for your answer.

122. Pictures

Summary

August's family are thrilled to see him at the reception afterwards. His extended family are there too, teary-eyed and wet-cheeked.

He poses with his friends for pictures, not even thinking about his face.

More and more kids come over for photos, laughing and squeezing in tight to get close to August.

Questions

1. What happens after the graduation ceremony?

2. How do August's family greet him?

3. "...for the first time I can remember, I wasn't even thinking about my face."
   Why has August forgotten about his face?
   How does this make you feel?

4. How does August feel as he gets his picture taken?

5. Is August having a good time?

6. What is the mood like at this point in the story?

123. The Walk Home

Summary

Afterwards, they walk through the beautiful June sunshine to August's for icecream.

August thanks his mom for sending him to school. She thanks him for being himself, a wonder in their lives.

Questions

1. What do they do after the reception?

2. What is the weather like?
   How does this add to the mood?

3. What sort of mood are the children in?

4. What does August say to his mom as they walk home?
   How does she reply?
   What does she mean here?
   How does this make you feel?

5. Is this a good ending?
   Explain your point of view.

124. Appendix

Summary

The appendix contains Mr. Browne's precepts for each month and those sent to him on postcards from students.

Questions

1. Which of Mr. Browne's precepts is your favourite? Explain your choice.

2. What similarities do you notice between these precepts?

3. Which of the Postcard Precepts is your favourite? Explain why it appeals to you.

Further Questions

1. Is this a book for adults or children?
   Explain your point of view.

2. Why has the author chosen to use multiple points of view to tell this story?

3. Do you like how this story is told?

4. Why, do you think, has the author decided to focus on this time in August's life?

5. There are no chapters from August's parents' perspectives. What would their story have added to this novel? Is the story missing something without their point of view?

6. What would chapters from Julian's and Eddie's point of view have added? Would they contribute anything positive to the story, do you think?

7. What problems do you foresee for August as he gets older? Do you think he will overcome these problems? Why/why not?

8. Is this a novel about growing up?

9. What does this novel teach us about maturity?

10. Is this a novel about accepting others?

11. Is this novel about accepting ourselves?

12. What is the author trying to show us in this story?

13. Did you enjoy the ending of this novel?
    Why/why not?
    Is it a fitting ending for the story?
    What questions are you left with?
    What sort of future do you imagine for August?

14. Do the characters in 'Wonder' lead happy lives?
    Refer to the text to support your ideas.

15. How is family life portrayed in this novel?
    Is this a realistic picture of family relationships, do you think?
    Does this picture of family life ring true?
    Refer to the text to support your ideas.

16. Is Auggie a good lead character?
    Give reasons for your answer.

17. Is Auggie a likeable character?
    Give reasons for your answer.

18. Is August a brave character?
    Explain your view.

19. Is Jack a brave character?
    Explain your view.

20. Who is your favourite character in the novel?
    What do you like about them?

21. Who is your least favourite character in the novel?
    What do you dislike about them?

22. What are the major themes and issues in this novel?
    How are they explored?
    What conclusions do you draw?

23. What did you enjoy about this story?

24. What did you dislike about this story?

25. Is this novel engaging and interesting?
    Explain your point of view.

26. Does this novel remind you of any novels you have read, or plays or films you have seen?
    Explain your point of view, including examples to support your view.

27. Does this story teach us anything about people?
    Does it teach us anything about life?
    Refer to the text to support the points you make.

www.ingramcontent.com/pod-product-compliance
Lightning Source LLC
Chambersburg PA
CBHW071224080526
44587CB00013BA/1488